Next World Conversations

Next World Conversations:

Reclaiming the Future, One Community at a Time

by Anna Willow and Terry Hermsen

(with the ROAR Collective)

Regional Ohio Action for Resilience

Regional Ohio Action for Resilience
Delaware, Ohio

©2022 Regional Ohio Action for Resilience

Library of Congress Publication Data
Authors: Willow, Anna J. | Hermsen, Terry
ISBN: 9780578370569 (print) | 9780578370576 (ebook)

Cover Photo Credit: Rijal Hafizh via Pixabay (free open license for
commercial use)

This book is for everyone
working to create a more sustainable,
resilient, and equitable world.

Next World Conversations would not be possible
without the involvement of numerous colleagues,
collaborators, and friends. Our roar is not the roar of lions.
It is the roar of bees. Thank you!

Contents

Next World Conversation Participants

Alyssa Battistoni (Chapter 9) is a political theorist with research interests in political economy, feminism, environmental and climate politics, Marxist thought, and the history of political ideas. Her current book project, *Free Gifts: Capitalism and the Politics of Nature*, draws on feminist and ecological thought to explore the representation of nature in capitalism. She is the co-author, with Kate Aronoff, Daniel Aldana Cohen, and Thea Riofrancos, of *A Planet to Win: Why We Need a Green New Deal* (Verso, 2019). Her work has appeared in *Political Theory, Perspectives on Politics, Contemporary Political Theory*, and *Nature Sustainability*. Battistoni also writes frequently for publications such as the *Nation, Dissent, Jacobin, n+1*, and *Boston Review*. She received her PhD from Yale and previously held the position of Environmental Fellow at Harvard University.

Dustin Braden (Chapter 6) is a recent graduate of Ohio Wesleyan University. Enthusiastic about pairing science with communications, Dustin got his start at Granville High School working with the Partners for Fish and Wildlife Program to restore approximately 35 acres of farmland into prairie and wetland habitat. Since then, he's worked at Ottawa National Wildlife Refuge and their nonprofit friends group to lead tours of public lands and increase their digital presence.

Kip Curtis (Chapter 3) is Associate Professor of Environmental History in the Ohio State University's Department of History and a 2020-2021 Faculty Fellow in the University Office of Outreach and Engagement. He has published on the history of mining and the history of environmental ideas, and is co-author of a forthcoming history of humans on earth. His current project focuses on a "history of the future" in which he imagines an urban food production system and then develops a grant to launch it. Working at the intersection of racial justice and ecologically-minded economic development, Curtis has partnered with the North End Community Improvement Collaborative and its Executive Director, Deanna West-Torrence, to launch a microfarming cooperative in Mansfield, Ohio that captures food dollars that once left the state and redirects them to local households and neighborhoods.

Jon-Paul d'Aversa (Chapter 4) was the senior energy planner with the Mid-Ohio Regional Planning Commission (MORPC) when this interview took place. Over the course of four years, he ensured a focus on energy and its impacts on public health across Central Ohio. Wanting to assist on a larger scale and geography, in May of 2021, d'Aversa created a firm called UNPREDICTABLEcity, which is dedicated to strengthening the foundations of change in our human systems. UNPREDICTABLEcity works with all levels of government, nonprofits, community groups, and the private sector to ensure we are remembered as good ancestors. Jon-Paul d'Aversa has been car-free for two years and counting. See www.unpredictable.city to learn more.

Reverend Marcia Dinkins (Chapter 7) is the Executive Director of Ohio Interfaith Power and Light. She has a background in organizing on issues related to domestic violence, health and safety, education, jobs, and crime reduction. Dinkins has worked at national, state, and local levels. She holds three degrees: Associate of Arts (Oakland Community College); Bachelor of Arts in Interdisciplinary and Women and Gender Studies (University of Toledo); and a Master of Arts in Criminal Justice and Policy (Youngstown State University). She has taught social justice workshops at Case Western University, Bowling Green State University, and the American Baptist Churches Leadership Academy.

Denise Fairchild (Chapter 5) is the inaugural President and CEO of Emerald Cities Collaborative (ECC), a national non-profit organization based in Washington, DC with affiliates in major urban centers across the United States. She is charged with advancing ECC's "high road" mission to green our cities, build resilient local economies, and ensure equity in both the processes and the outcomes of a new green and healthy economy. Dr. Fairchild focuses on building community-led partnerships with labor, environmental, and business organizations to increase energy efficiency, clean energy, sustainable foods, and clean water with a focus on low-income communities and communities of color. Her educational background includes degrees in urban planning from Fisk University, University of Pennsylvania, and a doctorate from UCLA. Her recent publication is entitled *Energy Democracy: Equity Solutions to the Clean Economy* (Island Press, 2017). She lives in and raised her family in South Los Angeles.

Terry Hermsen is Professor of English at Otterbein University. Hermsen taught in the Writers in the Schools program for the Ohio Arts Council from 1979-2003, visiting schools all across the state. He has conducted "poetry night hikes" in such places as Mohican State Park and Cuyahoga Valley National Park, as well as in California and Vermont. He now teaches English, Creative Writing, and Environmental Literature. Hermsen holds an MFA in Poetry from Goddard College and a PhD from Ohio State University in Art Education. His book, *The River's Daughter* (Bottom Dog Press), was co-recipient of the Ohio Poet of the Year Award in 2009. His most recent book of poems is called *A House for Last Year's Summer* (2017). His book on teaching poetry, *Poetry of Place*, was published by NCTE in 2009. In 2011 and 2012, Hermsen was co-director (and grant writer) for a teacher workshop in Cuyahoga Valley National Park called "Reading the Earth: The Language of Nature."

Pastor Shawn Jackson (Chapter 7) is the leader of Mayes Community Temple, located in Marion, Ohio. Jackson is also the Director of Student Life, Diversity, and Inclusion at the Ohio State University at Marion. Originally from Columbus, Jackson works to promote racial, economic, and environmental justice in his community and beyond.

Fadhel Kaboub (Chapter 5) is Associate Professor of Economics at Denison University and the president of the Global Institute for Sustainable Prosperity. He has also held research affiliations with the Levy Economics Institute, the John F. Kennedy School of Government at Harvard University, and the Economic Research Forum. He is an expert on Modern Monetary Theory, the Green New Deal, and the Job Guarantee. His work focuses on public policies to enhance monetary and economic sovereignty in the Global South, build resilience, and promote equitable and sustainable prosperity. His academic work has been published in numerous journals. His recent work has also been featured in the *New York Times, Financial Times, Bloomberg, Le Monde, Al Jazeera, France 24,* and *CGTN.* You can follow him on Twitter @FadhelKaboub and @GISP_Tweets.

Reed Kurtz (Chapter 9) is a Visiting Assistant Professor at Purdue University. His research focuses on Environmental Politics, International Relations, and Political Theory, with particular interests in the global politics of climate change. He is interested in exploring pathways and potential for radical political action and transformation in the face of global ecological crisis, including shifting state and civil society dynamics around the politics of climate governance and climate justice. Kurtz is currently writing and researching around questions regarding the role of direct action against climate change, exceptional politics and "climate emergency" discourse, and the future of global climate governance.

Randi Leppla (Chapter 4) is the Director of the Environmental Law Clinic at the Case Western Reserve University School of Law. Leppla previously served as the Ohio Environmental Council's Vice President of Energy Policy and Lead Energy Counsel, where she worked to advance clean energy and energy efficiency policies and projects, including working with utilities and businesses to create and implement plans for carbon pollution reduction. Prior to joining the OEC, Leppla was in private practice for several years. Her practice focused on litigation, natural gas utility issues, and utility-scale wind farm permitting. She holds a BA in Law, Letters, and Society from The University of Chicago and a JD from The Ohio State University's Michael E. Moritz College of Law.

David Orr (Chapter 8) is Paul Sears Distinguished Professor of Environmental Studies and Politics Emeritus and senior advisor to the president of Oberlin College. He is a founding editor of the journal *Solutions*, and founder of the Oberlin Project, a collaborative effort of the city of Oberlin, Oberlin College, and private and institutional partners to improve the resilience, prosperity, and sustainability of Oberlin. Orr is the author of eight books, including *Dangerous Years: Climate Change, the Long Emergency, and the Way Forward* (Yale, 2016) *and Down to the Wire: Confronting Climate Collapse* (Oxford, 2009), and coeditor of three others. He has authored over 200 articles, reviews, book chapters, and professional publications.

Jim Reding (Chapter 6) is a life science teacher, currently employed by the Granville Exempted Village Schools in Granville, Ohio. Along with teaching, he manages the garden and 100-acre "Land Lab" created by his students. He was selected as a Fulbright Scholar in 2009, received the Environmental Education Council of Ohio, Formal Educator of the year award in 2015, won the North American Association of Environmental Education Teacher of the Year award in 2016, and was awarded the Arthur S. Holden Teacher Award for Excellence in Science Education in 2017. He lives in Granville, Ohio with his wife and four kids. His hobbies are all outdoors.

Tim Van Meter (Chapter 3) is an Associate Professor at the Methodist Theological School in Ohio (MTSO) where he leads ecology and social justice specializations in the MDiv. MAPT, DMin, and the Master of Arts in Social Justice (MASJ) programs. He also serves as the campus Coordinator for Ecological Initiatives. MTSO has a ten-acre organic farm; a dining hall sourcing 85 percent from local, organic, and humane sources; a solar array and closed loop geothermal for primary academic buildings; and has hosted multiple events exploring ecology and interfaith dialogue. From 2017-2019, Van Meter served as the director of a grant from the Luce Fund for Theological Education supporting 1-3 day events on campuses across the US to increase ecological literacy in theological and religious higher education. From 2022-2027, he will lead a grant from the Lilly Endowment increasing pastoral literacy in the realm of ecology and religious literacy among ecological activists.

Joel Wainwright (Chapter 8) is Professor of Geography at the Ohio State University. He is the author of several books, including *Decolonizing Development: Colonial Power and the Maya* (Blackwell 2008); *Geopiracy: Oaxaca, Militant Empiricism, and Geographical Thought* (Palgrave 2012); and *Climate Leviathan: A Political Theory of our Planetary Future* (Verso, 2018, with Geoff Mann). Wainwright is also the editor of *Rethinking Palestine and Israel: Marxist Perspectives* (Routledge 2021, with Oded Nir).

Anna Willow is Professor of Anthropology at the Ohio State University. An environmental anthropologist who studies how individuals and communities experience and respond to externally imposed resource extractive development, she is the author of two books, including *Understanding ExtrACTIVISM: Culture and Power in Natural Resource Disputes* (Routledge, 2018) and *Strong Hearts, Native Lands: The Cultural and Political Landscape of Anishinaabe Anti-Clearcutting Activism* (SUNY, 2012). She is also the editor of *Anthropology and Activism: New Contexts, New Conversations* (Routledge, 2020) and *ExtrACTION: Impacts, Engagements, and Alternative Futures* (Routledge, 2017). Willow received her PhD in cultural anthropology in from the University of Wisconsin-Madison as well as a Master of Science in natural resources and environment from the University of Michigan.

1
Introduction

Times of crisis inspire visions of better worlds.

2020 will be remembered for the COVID-19 pandemic. As cities, states, and nations around the world instituted lockdowns to slow the novel virus's spread, both the density of our global interconnections and the inseparability of public health, economic stability, and emotional wellbeing became impossible to ignore. For many, COVID-19 was a global crisis that became profoundly personal; we erased anticipated life events from calendars, scrambled to supplement lost incomes, and grieved for those who died before their time. The dramatic action taken in response to the pandemic made it feel like the very real emergency it was.

For environmentally concerned citizens, however, the rapid reaction to COVID-19 threw world political and business leaders' refusal to address the unfolding emergencies of climate change and ecological decline into immediate relief. When media reports commended the temporary drop in greenhouse gas emissions that resulted from covid-related travel restrictions (Henriques 2020), we were reminded of the grim reality that climate change will ultimately kill exponentially more people than the present virus. When celebrities candidly role modeled the "new normal" of home quarantine and decision-makers caved to vehement demands to return to business as usual, we paused to ponder how we could live differently. We counted blessings and celebrated silver linings. And, as we struggled to make sense of it all, we realized that the "old normal" we had left behind was very deeply flawed. We will not go back.

We are living in an era of multiple, converging crises. The sixth great extinction is underway, with an unprecedented number of species projected to be lost within our lifetimes (Díaz et al. 2019; Ceballos et al.

2020). We are approaching—or have surpassed—numerous critical ecological thresholds (Steffen et al. 2015). And the stable climate our predecessors took for granted is now changing rapidly, bringing rising sea levels and extreme weather events (IPCC 2018). Generations of unsustainable development caused these problems, and none of us are immune to their effects. Both literally and figuratively, the most vulnerable populations are already facing the fiercest storms. Such was the case with COVID-19, as Black, Latinx, and Indigenous Americans died of the disease at far higher rates than their white counterparts (Ford et al. 2020; Wu et al. 2020). Systemic injustice—manifested as chronic lack of access to healthcare, nutritious food, and clean air—is to blame (Perron and Gross 2020). The public rage that erupted following the murders of George Floyd, Breonna Taylor, and too many others in the summer of 2020 was underlain by a bottomless sea of frustration fomented by the same inequitable structures. Hurricanes lined up in the Gulf of Mexico and fires ravaged the West. The news from other parts of the world was equally troubling. It felt like everything was wrong.

Required to rethink our everyday lives and witness to ongoing tragedies that no longer seemed separable, we came to regard the tribulations of that cruel year as symptoms of the slower-moving, intersecting catastrophes of income inequality, political dysfunction, and the relentless abuse of our planet. Our world, we realized, was already in crisis. In the words of activist author Naomi Klein, we have been "sleepwalking toward apocalypse" (2019:229). It is time to wake up. It is clear that the "old normal" that delivered us to this point—the status quo of unsustainable overconsumption, ecological disconnection, and short-sighted-self-centeredness—will not carry us beyond it. As the number of people adversely impacted by conjoined social and environmental crises steadily increases, so too does the space between the world we currently inhabit and the world that *could* be. Intensely aware of the gap between real and ideal and equally uncertain how to bridge it, our time of crisis is a "utopian moment" (Lockyer and Veteto 2013:1), a chance to strive for something better. But what comes next? How are better worlds made? And where do we begin?

Next World Conversations arose out of heartfelt discussions among friends and collaborators in March and April of 2020. Those at the center of Regional Ohio Action for Resilience (ROAR) confronted the same question as millions of families, campuses, businesses, and organizations: What now?

Based in Delaware, Ohio—a 40,000 resident outer-ring suburb of Columbus—ROAR brings individuals and groups together to facilitate climate and sustainability action. Grand plans to launch intersectional working groups around food, energy, natural areas, and community outreach went into hiatus with the widespread pandemic pause. After a few weeks of quiet introspection, this volume's curators came together to discuss what we might be able to accomplish in our unanticipated new circumstances. We wanted to do something that matched the current collective mood and reflected what so many of us seemed to be thinking. And so, we asked a select group of experts to join us for a series of live online conversations in which we talked and thought deeply about the future of food, energy, economies, education, justice, democracy, and our changing climate. Selections from these conversations are presented in the chapters that follow. We also met with a talented group of high school students from Granville, Ohio, who offered their own distinctive perspectives on many of these topics. Their words are featured in textboxes at the end of each chapter.

As challenging as those early covid seasons were, we chose to reframe the closures, systemic shocks, and public unrest as an opportunity to bring something better into being. Sent to our homes and stripped of our conveniences, we learned the vital lesson that we can live differently. It doesn't have to be like this! Change is possible! We look forward to the next world and invite you to participate in its creation. Truth be told, change is inevitable. Even if we succeed in preventing the most catastrophic effects of climate change and ecological collapse, future generations will experience a physical reality far less forgiving than our own. They will contend with greatly-reduced energy flows and significant civilizational shifts. Prominent environmental thinker David

Fleming argued that these impending socioecological transformations will "leave nothing in our lives unchanged" (2016:5). Our job, he declared, is not to prevent the crash, but rather to "develop the skills, the will and the resources necessary to recapture the initiative and build the resilient sequel to our present society" (Fleming 2016:8).

Given uncountable unknowns, it is natural to be inspired by fear. In our darkest moments, many of us envision a future that resembles nothing so much as a dystopian horror film. But running from a future we fear leaves us directionless. We need somewhere to run, something to strive for. This is the ultimate goal of *Next World Conversations*. In our small corner of the world, we are developing positive visions of the possible. We are building a stronger, healthier, more sustainable, and more equitable community one small step at a time. If we can do it, you can too. This volume offers inspiring places to start; the visions you generate—and the directions you take—are yours and yours alone.

Emergency and emergence are part of the same process. Rebecca Solnit reminds us of the words' shared Latin origin: "*Emergency* comes from *emerge*, to rise out of, the opposite of merge," she notes, which in turn comes from the term *mergere*, meaning "to be within or under a liquid, immersed, submerged" (2009:10). Much has been spoken and written about our state of immersion. In this volume, we contemplate how we will rise. We believe that successfully surmounting the long- and short-emergencies of our troubled times will require three interrelated abilities:

❖ First, *we need the capacity to imagine other, better worlds.* Rob Hopkins, founder of the Transition movement for climate change resilience, was surprised to find that many visionary authors (Paolo Lugari, Amitav Ghosh, George Monibot, and David Wallace-Wells among them) describe the climate crisis not as a technical or energy crisis but as a failure of *imagination* (Hopkins 2019). Today, too many people are unable to conceive of a world not powered by fossil fuels, of a valuation system not dominated by financial capital, of a life lived differently. We have forgotten how to dream.

As Hopkins sees it, only if we push ourselves to actively imagine a better world will we conjure the energy and determination necessary to bring that world into being.

❖ Second, *we need to believe that these worlds are possible.* We need examples—from far and near, past and present—compelling enough to convince ourselves and others that utopian strivings are more than just entertainment. Anthropological futurist Samuel Gerald Collins contends that the other worlds we imagine are not merely possible but are "virtualities waiting to be actualized" (2007:122). As social scientists, humanitarians, community leaders, and communicators, it is our job to bring these virtualities to light.

❖ Third, *we need to trust in our capacity to bring a better world into being.* Narratives about where we've been and what we might become matter. We have the power to shift the dominant narrative about our collective past, present, and future by telling hopeful new stories about human trajectories and possibilities (Bruner 1986). In 2009, Aleut scholar Eve Tuck called on Indigenous peoples to suspend the long tradition of "damage-centered research" (2009:409) that depicted their communities as riddled with pathology and loss. Her key directive to "stop thinking of ourselves as broken" (Tuck 2009:409) has relevance far beyond her original audience. For the millions of concerned world citizens who despair over what the future will bring and for the large portion of young people who now say that life is not worth living (Hine 2019), elevating instances of success and cultivating "applied optimism" (Hopkins 2008:15) is an urgent undertaking.

Imagination. Possibility. Efficacy. While these words may sound simple, these individual and collective capacities form the foundation on which positive futures are built. If we are unable to imagine better worlds, don't believe they are possible, and don't think our actions matter, the next world may turn out to be a very dark place. The reality is that even as some among us envision positive post-carbon futures, very powerful forces—forces like fossil fuel companies and governments beholden to them—will continue to advocate contrasting visions of what tomorrow could bring. If we lack foresight and direction, we have already lost. Many of us wrestle with moments (or months) of pessimism, but people separated by time and space have repeatedly proven that "striving for a better world is a fundamentally human condition" (Lockyer and Veteto 2013:20). *Next World Conversations* contributes, humbly, to this enduring quest.

Everything, as we know it right now,
isn't working.
Since there is no correct answer, it's
up to us to figure out what's going to
work and what isn't.
                ~John, 10th Grade

2
How Better Worlds Are Made: A Glossary For Change

Strategies for building better worlds are as diverse as our vocabularies for talking about them. Recent decades have given us a multitude of inspiring options. In this chapter, we offer an annotated glossary—organized conceptually rather than alphabetically—of relevant terms and concepts. Countless additional opportunities for making change are described in the chapters and conversations that follow.

Utopianism~
the transformation of generalized hope
into the description of a non-existent society

As a literary genre, utopianism emerged in 1516 with the publication of Sir Thomas More's *Utopia*. But long before that, people talked, daydreamed, and created great mythologies about superior (yet seemingly unattainable) states of being. Utopias are fictional societies that express the ideals of their inventors. Utopia is simultaneously a "good" place and, as the term's Greek origins attest, "no place" (*eu*topia) at all. The quest for utopia is part of being human. As Lyman Sargent observes, "people have always been dissatisfied with the conditions of their lives and have created visions of a better and longer life and hoped for a continued and improved existence after death" (Sargent 2010:4). Indeed, most cultures around the world boast a strong utopian tradition, tailored to culturally specific conceptions of what an ideal reality implies.

Utopias translate our hopes for the future into compelling descriptions of better, richer modes of everyday life that do not (yet) exist. They transform generalized hope into descriptions of non-existent societies (Sargent 2010:8) and "produce a vision of a good elsewhere or elsewhen that projects from the present into somewhere and somewhen other than the spatial-temporal here and now" (Anderson 2006:702). Utopian visions are inherently diverse and dynamic. While the notion of utopia as a "blueprint" to implement has been roundly critiqued as potentially repressive and politically charged, most recent thinkers celebrate utopia as an experimental and open-ended process. Recognizing that one person's paradise may be another's nightmare, contemporary utopianism emphasizes the pull of the possible rather than any given endpoint (Carspecken 2012). So, too, is the search for utopia acknowledged as an endless quest, with visions of better worlds shifting and expanding as soon as one goal is achieved (Sargent 2010).

Utopianism peaks in times of struggle, among groups experiencing hardship or oppression. In periods of economic, political, and social strife, citizens become acutely aware that their circumstances could be significantly improved. As the distance between "here" and "there" increases, utopianism abounds (Pepper 2005). It is this distance that both inspires utopian thinking and elevates its potency as a form of radical critique. Feminist theorist Lucy Sargisson uses the term *estrangement* to capture the conceptual value of such distance. Set apart in time and/or space, utopia is able to tell a different story; it "breaks rules that constrain the present; it thinks the unthinkable" (Sargisson 2007:395). Utopias function as a "thought experiment" in which we imagine what it is like to exist otherwise (Harvey 2000). They transport us (however temporarily) to a distant realm and oblige us to see through new eyes upon our return (Anderson 2006).

Even when particular versions of utopia do not suit our fancy and stand no chance of being realized, utopianism forces us to ask "what if" questions and consider what life *could* be like (Carspecken 2012:55). As demonstrated by the popularity of modern science fiction and fantasy, descriptions of other worlds have enormous appeal. By toppling the taken-for-granted and daring us to dream, utopianism inspires visions of more fulfilling worlds, whether those worlds are unmistakably fictional or compellingly realistic. Occasionally, people found intentional communities or launch social movements that attempt to turn utopian visions into reality (Sargent 2010). (Ecotopian imaginings, to cite one relevant example, provide impetus for ecovillages and similar experiments in sustainable individual and communal living (Pepper 2005)). By celebrating the generative power of imagination, utopianism reminds us that better worlds are possible— an essential prerequisite for bringing such worlds to light.

Intentional communities~
communities founded for the explicit purpose of achieving specific social and cultural goals

When you picture an intentional community, you likely envision a group of people who choose to live together or maintain common facilities because of mutually and explicitly shared values. These kinds of communities do exist: They range from religious communities, to urban cohousing initiatives, to ecovillages. But intentional communities can also be defined more broadly to encompass groups that "share values, physical space, and resources" or even organizations that manage pooled resources for "a group of people with a shared mission or purpose" (Foundation for Intentional Community 2019). While intentional communities may look diverse, they are all "purposely and voluntarily founded to achieve a specific goal for a specific group of people bent on solving a specific set of cultural and social problems" (Brown 2002a:5). Their members agree on fundamental values and opt to work together to build a better world (usually on a small, manageable scale). Such communities need not be geographically emplaced. They can also be "communities of spirit" that cut across space and time to forge common histories, practices, understandings, and identities (Brown 2002a:3).

Intentional communities are not a new phenomenon. Throughout history—especially in periods of extreme stress, rapid change, and cultural confusion—people have come together with the aim of creating a reality that better matches their ideal (Brown 2002a). Such communities simultaneously express a movement *toward* an alternative mode of living and *away* from a mode of living that participants perceive as problematic (Carspecken 2012). When intentional community members elect to live differently and/or separately from mainstream society, they implicitly challenge existing patterns of social and ecological interaction—a fact not lost on defenders of the status quo who tend to perceive intentional communities as threatening (Metcalf 2012). While an accurate count is impossible, thousands of intentional communities—of all shapes and sizes and in all regions of the world—exist today.

A clear line can be drawn between utopian thinking and intentional communities. As utopian studies scholar Lyman Sargent explains, "the most common form of putting a specific vision into practice has been to create a small community either to withdraw from the larger society to practice the beliefs of its members without interference or to demonstrate to the larger society that their utopia could be put into practice" (2010:33). Intentional communities are real world places where people attempt to realize ideals. They are concrete manifestations of utopian visions, "spaces in which the good life is explored and pursued" while evaluating dominant social structures from a distant—and ostensibly better—place (Sargisson 2007:393). In addition to providing their members with a platform for social critique and a collection of tangible alternatives, intentional communities have value for society as a whole; they model new ways of living and expand the range of acceptable options. Intentional communities are thus a powerful force for social change (Carspeken 2012).

Ecovillages~
intentional communities founded with the goal of establishing an ecologically sustainable way of life

Ecovillages are "intentional communities that use integrative design, local economic networking, cooperative and common property structures, and participatory decision making to minimize ecological footprints and provide as many of life's basic necessities as possible in a sustainable manner" (Lockyer and Veteto 2013:15). Like other intentional communities, they are purposeful expressions of their founders' shared values and goals. In this case, the desire to protect the Earth and live in an ecologically sustainable manner is first and foremost. As physical expressions of environmental convictions, ecovillages are living laboratories for the creation of alternative political ecologies (Burke and Arjona 2013). The physical characteristics of ecovillages (e.g., renewable energy installations, buildings constructed of natural/local materials, organic gardens, composting toilets, rainwater catchment) and the actions of their members (e.g., car sharing, repurposing of materials, use of communal shower and laundry facilities) (Boyer 2016; Lockyer 2017) demonstrate the continuing capacity of people to integrate into their natural surroundings in a sustainable, harmonious, and resilient manner.

Prefiguration~
undertaking actions and constructing relationships that model the changes one wishes to create

Prefiguration is a social movement strategy in which participants act in ways that foreshadow the changes they seek to create. Such actions demonstrate to movement participants and outsiders alike that change is possible. According to Marianne Maeckelbergh, prefiguration is a conscious decision to achieve goals using processes that embody those goals. Practicing prefiguration thus implies "removing the temporal distinction between the struggle in the present and a goal in the future; instead, the struggle and the goal, the real and the ideal, become one in the present" (Maeckelbergh 2011:4). Purposefully providing examples of the other worlds they would like to see realized, participants in prefigurative movements develop egalitarian social structures, build communities, and reinvent political ecologies—often in parallel with other forms of social protest (Maeckelbergh 2009; Yates 2015). In this way, prefiguration circumvents the glacial pace of progress that so often stymies significant social change. Refusing to defer change to a later date while policy reforms or political processes play out, prefigurative movements create the future *in* the present (Sitrin 2006). Like intentional communities and nowtopias, prefiguration represents an attempt to create a better world not in a distant someday, but in the here and now.

Everyday activism~
commitment to social, ecological, and political change expressed through individual daily actions

As time passes and social and ecological crises worsen, increasing numbers of individuals have come to realize that conventional political channels of protest and policy intervention are either insufficient or altogether ineffective. Instead of expecting the system that created these problems to resolve them, everyday activists go beyond critique to enact solutions on a tangible and manageable scale. Political theorist Jane Mansbridge coined the phrase *everyday activism* to describe "talk and action in everyday life that is not consciously coordinated with the actions of others but is (1) to some degree caused (inspired, encouraged) by a social movement and (2) consciously intended to change others' ideas of behavior in directions advocated by the movement" (2012:437-8).

Within the environmental arena, everyday activism takes multiple forms. People express their broad desire to create more sustainable flows of energy and materials through human and nonhuman communities by participating in food movements (i.e., slow food, food justice, and urban agriculture), cooperative energy generation, repurposing, and crafting. As David Schlosberg and Romand Coles indicate, these movements represent "a new politics of sustainable materialism, an environmentalism of everyday life" (2016:161). By choosing to meet quotidian needs in a more sustainable—and often more fulfilling—way, everyday activists reject problematic practices individually while also working to reconstruct collective institutions.

Drawing on precedents in the environmental justice movement (in which the impacts of degraded environments on human bodies and material circumstances have been a central focus), the environmentalism of everyday life seeks just and sustainable options for meeting basic human needs (Agyeman et al. 2016). It calls on individuals to "confront power by stepping out of existing flows of materials and capital [and] by embodying alternatives rather than just supporting values, policies, or candidates" (Schlosberg and Coles 2016:178). In contrast to the flamboyant activism of public protest, everyday activists resist extractivist human-environment relationships, unjust social structures, and consumerist values by making changes in their daily lives. Simultaneously more subtle and more radical than conventional activism, everyday activists choose to live differently and encourage others to join them.

Nowtopias~
finding liberation in work done for social and ecological reasons rather than for the proliferation of capital

Nowtopias are practical projects undertaken by people who refuse to wait for a better life. The term refers to "work that is done for social and ecological reasons and explicitly *not* for the proliferation of capital" (Carlsson and Manning 2010:928). Nowtopias take a wide range of forms, all which decouple wellbeing from wealth and consumption. Many Nowtopian projects are concrete and relatively labor intensive— common examples include vacant lot (also known as guerrilla) gardening, "outlaw" bicycling for transportation and togetherness, and free computer software programming (Carlsson 2008). But Nowtopians come from many segments of society and include not only rebellious youth but also elderly retirees. As Mary Gearey and Neil Ravenscroft note, "there are a plethora of ordinary, pedestrian, low visibility Nowtopian practices burgeoning in unrecognized corners" (2019:462). Wherever and however they proceed, Nowtopians engage in tangible projects they see as "worthwhile, fulfilling, and necessary" (Gearey and Ravenscroft 2019:454). The fact that they are unpaid for their labor is significant. Nowtopians insist that their worth cannot be measured in the amount of their paycheck and seek to liberate themselves from the class structure by forming "identities, communities, and meaning outside of paid work" (Carlsson 2008:42).

The utopian impulse is expressed in myriad ways, many of them modest or ephemeral (Sargent 2010:33). Nowtopians build their own small versions of utopia in their own communities. "Nowtopia, like Utopia, is a "no place," but unlike Utopia, it is also an "everywhere,"" writes Chris Carlsson in his seminal book on the topic. "It is appealing to imagine a harmonious and peaceful transition to a sensible, humane, and comfortable life for everyone," Carlsson adds, and "Nowtopian efforts are always, consciously or not, working in that direction" (2008:252). Nowtopians recognize the importance of their own actions in creating the world they inhabit. Instead of allowing that world to be a degrading and demoralizing one, they choose to work together, here and now, to create something better.

Cultural revitalization~
a deliberate, organized, conscious effort by members of a society to construct a more satisfying culture

Around the world and for thousands of years, communities have found ways to increase their members' wellbeing by transforming their values, expectations, and ways of life. In the mid-twentieth century, Anthony F.C. Wallace noticed that societies ranging from seventh century Arabia to nineteenth century Native North America followed a familiar pattern in responding to environmental, economic, and political pressures. When new challenges arise, customary coping mechanisms become inadequate. As the mismatch between problems and solutions intensifies, people start to see their cultural system as unsatisfactory. They attempt to relieve the resulting anxiety both by transforming their conceptions of self and society and by working to change the system that surrounds them. Wallace famously termed these collective responses *cultural revitalization movements*, which he defined as "deliberate, organized, conscious effort[s] by members of a society to construct a more satisfying culture" (1956:265). Anthropologists, historians, and ethnohistorians use the cultural revitalization framework to think processually about how better worlds are made.

Most of the cultural revitalization movements documented by Wallace and his colleagues occurred in the nineteenth and early twentieth centuries among recently colonized Indigenous peoples in North America and the Pacific Islands. While cultural revitalization can be catalyzed by biological (epidemic disease, famine, malnutrition) or environmental (environmental degradation, climatic change, natural disasters) catastrophes, these prominent cases were triggered by politically asymmetrical colonial encounters. As a result, scholars have often argued that cultural revitalization movements are "strategies to gain power" (McMullen 2004:261) relative to a dominant and encompassing society. While this point remains relevant, cultural revitalization movements are not only long-ago and far-away (Wallace 2004).

In the decades following the Great Acceleration (the rapid intensification of humanity's impacts on the Earth and its systems that began around 1950 (Steffen et al. 2015)), more and more members of Western industrial societies came to the alarming realization that the environment that sustains us is not infinite. This, coupled with the concomitant revelation that activities that degrade the environment do not necessarily deliver additional happiness, led to existential and emotional stress and a mounting sense of cultural dissatisfaction. Today, amidst profound angst precipitated by climate change and ecological decline, deep dissatisfaction with individualistic/consumerist value structures, and widespread hopelessness, cultural revitalization movements continue to arise as people come together to create more satisfying cultural alternatives. New religious movements (e.g., Lee 1996; Robbins 2004) and holistic environmental/cultural movements can be fruitfully examined through this lens (e.g., Willow 2021). While inspired by internal disagreements between members of the same complex society regarding fundamental values, assumptions about the future, and how to respond to socioecological crises rather than by explicit intersocietal inequity, participants in these movements deploy revitalization as a conscious act of resistance and a form of cultural critique (Brown 2002b). Contemporary cultural revitalization movements thus emerge as strategies to overcome anxiety, promote positive futures, resist dominant but damaging societal status quos, and provide hope to those who need it most.

Disaster communities~
the sense of solidarity and possibility that ensues when the status quo is upended by catastrophe

In *A Paradise Built in Hell*, Rebecca Solnit reminds us of the tightknit communities and social solidarity that often form following natural or man-made disasters. Solnit is careful not to celebrate the disasters themselves (her case studies cover earthquakes and hurricanes, explosions and fires). The disasters are not the gifts, she writes, "they are one avenue through which the gifts arrive" (Solnit 2009:6). The value of these events lies in people's responses to them. Disasters upend the normal social order. When systemic failures and inequities that we typically take for granted are temporarily suspended, we realize that things could be otherwise. Forced by catastrophe to live and think differently, we realize that transforming the status quo is a realistic possibility. "It is the disruptive power of disaster that matters here," Solnit explains, "the ability of disasters to topple old orders and open new possibilities" (2009:16).

The climate crisis, ecological decline, and massive social inequity loom large among the problems that now lead many concerned citizens to feel trapped in perpetual disaster. Solnit's ideas offer clues as to how we might proceed. Most people, it turns out, do not thrive under conditions of secure tranquility; rather, we rise to our fullest potential when given a sense of purpose, a feeling that we are "struggling toward a worthwhile goal" (Solnit 2009:97). Recognizing our daily disaster for what it is means acknowledging that our systems are not working. Disaster communities demonstrate that we can remake the shattered world around us. They impel us to identify—and then struggle together to achieve—a diverse range of worthwhile goals.

Degrowth~
a project to challenge the hegemony of economic growth in order to achieve environmental sustainability, social justice, and holistic wellbeing

The degrowth movement emerged in the 1970s, disseminating from France (where it is called *décroissance*) to academic and activist circles around Mediterranean Europe. Despite conceptual precedents in E.F. Schumacher's *Small is Beautiful* (1973) and the *Limits to Growth* report (Meadows et al. 1972), it was not until 2008—the year of both the first international degrowth conference and the most severe economic recession since the Great Depression—that the concept gained traction in the Anglophone literature. The main premise of Degrowth is simple: Societies are not destined to either "grow or die." Sustainable sufficiency and holistic wellbeing can replace endless growth and material accumulation as key indices of progress and prosperity.

The goal of Degrowth is not to create a greener or more inclusive capitalist system, but to build a system that is altogether different (Demaria et al. 2019). Proponents argue that Degrowth is not just about using less. Rather, it is about a new way of living—a life of simplicity and frugal abundance in communities shaped by collaboration and deep democracy. According to Federico Demaria and Serge Latouche, two of the movement's leading architects, everything from energy sources to gender roles will be different in a degrowth society (Demaria and Latouche 2019:148). Recognizing the resource overshoot and ecological devastation intrinsic to growth-obsessed economies as well as the injustice (both within and between world regions) that such systems produce, Degrowth "challenges the hegemony of growth and calls for a democratically led redistributive downscaling of production and consumption in industrialised countries as a means to achieve environmental sustainability, social justice and well-being" (Demaria et al. 2013:209). As of this writing, there are 114 active Degrowth initiatives in Europe and beyond.

Buen Vivir~
a social philosophy advocating good living through collectivity, decolonization, and harmonious coexistence

Taken literally, *Buen Vivir* means "good living" or "living well." But unlike Western notions of wellbeing or "the good life," Buen Vivir expresses and cultivates a deep transformation in adherents' knowledge, affectivity, and spiritual reality along with a new understanding of relationships between humans and non-humans (Chuji et al. 2019:111). A work in progress rather than an organized social movement, Buen Vivir combines critiques of the economic growth imperative with South American Indigenous teachings surrounding the intrinsic value of non-human nature. Described by key proponents as "a concept under construction that aspires to go beyond conventional development," Buen Vivir is a social philosophy advocating good living through collectivity, decolonization, and harmonious coexistence (Gudynas and Acosta 2011:70).

Many observers view Buen Vivir as a Southern complement to Degrowth. But calls to reduce consumption make little sense for residents of the global South who have never had the opportunity to consume more than their share of planetary resources. While both projects agree that capitalism's demand for endless economic growth is detrimental to life on Earth and must be replaced with a more relational, sustainable, and participatory philosophy (Gudynas 2011), Buen Vivir enriches Degrowth's rejection of growth, development, and material measures of prosperity with substantive spiritual and intercultural dimensions.

Biophilia~
the urge to affiliate with other forms of life

Biophilia means "love of life." Renowned biologist Edward O. Wilson popularized the term in his eponymously titled book, suggesting that humans possess an innate urge to affiliate with other forms of life (Wilson 1984:85). Since then, the concept has proven influential in the disparate realms of design, psychology, and education. Celebrating organic forms and cultivating attachment to place, biophilic design represents the deliberate attempt to incorporate elements of the natural world into built environments in order to enhance human health and productivity (Kellert 2011). Going beyond more conventional discussions of sustainable, green, or low-impact design, biophilic design sets out to reconnect people with the natural world. The need to reconnect with nature has also been noted by ecopsychologists and environmental education proponents who respectively argue that ecological connection is necessary for emotional wellbeing (Roszak 2001) and that connection to nature is essential for children's mental, physical, and spiritual development (Louv 2008).

Permaculture~
the conscious design and maintenance of agriculturally productive ecosystems that have the diversity, stability, and resilience of natural ecosystems

Permaculture is a system of holistic landscape design, but it is also much more. It is a way of working the land underlain by a philosophy of interconnection and sustainability. As implied by the combination of words that comprise the term, permaculture strives to create a permanent agriculture and a culture capable of sustaining itself over time. Permaculture originated in Australia in the 1970s and subsequently became known around the world through books published by Bill Mollison and David Holmgren. In his foundational *Permaculture: A Designer's Manual*, Mollison defines permaculture as "the conscious design and maintenance of agriculturally productive ecosystems which have the diversity, stability, and resilience of natural ecosystems" (Mollison 1988:ix). Permaculture accepts a wide range of influences—ranging from Indigenous agricultural techniques to Western science—that facilitate its goal of carefully observing and learning from the natural world. According to Erik Ohlsen, a California-based permaculture designer and author, "permaculture is a system of change that constantly adapts and grows on its own" (quoted in Carlsson 2008:75). Permaculture recognizes the natural world (and our relationships within that world) as dynamic and cyclical; in this context, cooperation and adaptation are essential capacities.

Given permaculture's holistic and forward-looking vision, proponents see it as a promising tool for converting sustainable ideals into on-the-ground realities. Permaculture, posit Lockyer and Veteto, "is an ecotopian methodology" (2013:11). It requires thinking that goes far beyond Western industrial society's self-centered, short-term conceptual horizon. The call to think broadly and act accordingly is clearly discernable in permaculture's core principles, which are outlined in David Holmgren's *Permaculture: Principles and Pathways Beyond Sustainability* (2010):

- Observe and interact
- Catch and store energy
- Obtain a yield
- Apply self-regulation and accept feedback
- Use and value renewable resources and services
- Produce no waste
- Design from patterns to details
- Integrate rather than segregate
- Use small and slow solutions
- Use and value diversity
- Use edges and value the marginal
- Creatively use and respond to change

While these principles can be interpreted literally in the context of agricultural production, they are just as frequently celebrated as ethical guidelines for living sustainably, making permaculture a guiding force in movements ranging from regenerative agriculture (see chapter 3) to Transition.

Transition~
an international movement to build local resilience
in anticipation of climate change and fossil fuel scarcity

Transition is a global "movement of movements" that promotes local resilience in anticipation of climate change and fossil fuel scarcity. Transition originated in 2005-2006, when permaculture students in Kinsale, Ireland and Totnes, England began exploring the possibility of a proactive descent from fossil fuel dependency (Hopkins 2011). From there, the idea spread rapidly. Today, Transition is a loosely integrated international movement with over one thousand official registered groups (and countless unofficial ones) in forty-three countries around the world (with concentrations in Europe, North America, and Australia).

Even as it addresses the quintessential twenty-first century environmental issues of climate change and resource depletion, several interrelated attributes make Transition unique among environmental initiatives. First, Transition is self-organizing. Described by its founder as "a social experiment on a huge scale" (Hopkins 2013:48), Transition is designed to spread horizontally and take on the characteristics of its communities of emergence (Biddau et al. 2016; Felicetti 2017). Transition celebrates relocalization and emplacement while simultaneously enabling small local groups to tap into a rich global network. Second, by encouraging simple, material responses to monumental geopolitical problems, Transition crosses scales to make positive change seem possible (Martindale 2015). Profoundly skeptical about what top-down processes can achieve, Transition is not a protest movement in any conventional sense but rather empowers participants to determine their communities' destiny through practical here-and-now action (Henfrey and Kendrick 2015).

Third, Transition is distinguished by its positive tone. While environmentalists are often critiqued as purveyors of doom-and-gloom, Transition regards our current crisis "not as a cause for despair but as a transformational opportunity, a prospective change for the better that should be embraced rather than feared" (Alexander and Gleeson 2019:106). This optimistic stance has been welcomed by citizens seeking to respond constructively to the social and ecological challenges we now face. Finally (and most significantly), Transition is distinguished by its explicit call to change and generate culture. As Emily Polk discovered during her work with Transition Amherst (Massachusetts), Transition is about moving "from one ideology to another" (2015:92). Members of individual Transition groups work locally to create a more satisfying way of life confident that analogous action is underway elsewhere. In so doing, they overcome the despair and anxiety evoked by the realization that Western industrial culture is no longer tenable.

These ideas—all of them and more of them—will help us travel from the troubled circumstances that currently surround us to the better worlds we are working to create. In this necessarily incomplete glossary, we recognize many of our own ideals and actions. We suspect that you also see your yearnings reflected here, even if the labels and language are unfamiliar. While these entries offer inspiring possibilities, they are far from the only avenues for taking action. As we see it, this volume is also activism of a sort. It is not meant to be read and returned to a lonely shelf. It is action taken to encourage action. Its life exists outside of its pages. Rebecca Solnit writes that "every activist movement begins by uniting its participants in important ways, giving them a sense of purpose drawn from the wrongs they seek to right and the shared vision of a better world" (2009:285). If the words we have gathered contribute to a collective sense of purpose and clear new paths toward promising tomorrows, we will have succeeded beyond our wildest dreams.

In *Spaces of Hope*, David Harvey proclaims that people desperately need spaces where life is lived differently (2000). These spaces may be dance halls, community gardens, or festival grounds—any experienced time in place that reminds us that we are not locked into one mode of being. We need spaces where our imaginations run free, times when we allow ourselves to believe that life could be better. *Next World Conversations* is such a space. In the conversations we hosted between June 25, 2020 and January 7, 2021, innovative thinkers joined us to dream—grandly and publicly—about what the next world could bring. The chapters you are about to read offer tastes of what such a world could look like. More importantly, however, they are meant to inspire *your* visions of better days ahead. By the end of her career, famed anthropologist Margaret Mead was convinced that "how hard we are willing to work for the future depends largely upon our image of what that future will be like." As she explained,

> "if we take the pessimistic view that human nature is
> getting progressively worse and our future will be grim,
> it is tempting to just give up, refuse to bring more

children into the world, and to live out our lives consuming all the gasoline we can. If, on the other hand, we feel that it *is* possible to master our present-day problems, we can summon up the dedication and political will necessary to create a better world" (Mead 2005:331).

We owe it to future generations not to give in to pessimism. Instead of lamenting that everything is wrong, we choose to concentrate on what we can make right. We have a lot of work to do: We need new economic and political arrangements, new relationships with one another and with non-human nature, new moral institutions, and new problem-solving processes. At the same time, it behooves us to pause and consider which vestiges of the "old world" we wish to keep. In recent years, many of us have realized that when it comes to addressing climate change, environmental quality, and human wellbeing, those in positions of power are too often incapable of initiating significant change or uninterested in doing so. We have to do it ourselves. Right here, right now. Let's begin.

---

*Listen and be open-minded about new ideas and things
changing instead of trying to keep everything the same.
Make small sacrifices so that future generations don't have to
make bigger sacrifices. Everyone doing something
small will make a huge impact.*
~Ella, 11th Grade

*A lot of adults can recognize that putting their house on green
energy or starting to recycle is good, but a lot of them think,
"if I'm the only one doing it, it doesn't change anything."*
Take that leap of faith!
*Even if you think your small contribution won't matter,
if enough people start adopting that mindset, then it will.*
~George, 11th Grade

3
Local Food and the Future of Agriculture

Food connects us to the world beyond ourselves. Every time we eat or drink, we bring small pieces of the non-human realm not only into our daily lives but into our very bodies. Plants and (for many of us) animals provide the essential energy we need to survive, the energy that enables us to act within and upon our world. While citizens of industrial societies often overlook these realities, it cannot be otherwise. Food is an "inescapable ecology" (Nash 2006) that binds us to the dynamic natural systems apart from which we cannot exist. Food also ties us to other human beings in extraordinary ways. Every bite you take was produced somewhere and by someone, yet we rarely pause to consider where and who, or to trace how our food traveled from there to here. When we do attempt to answer these questions, the relationships between food and countless other systems become readily apparent: Fuel is used to produce food and transport it, economic arrangements determine who can access nutritious food and how, and political structures empower some individuals to make these decisions. So too do we find that food can bring us together, with school gardens nourishing educational growth and community gardens yielding social relationships as bountiful as their crops. Before and beyond the ways it aligns with energy, economics, social justice, education, and community cohesion, food also has enormous effects on global ecosystems and climates. In cyclical fashion, these biogeophysical impacts return home to influence our lives.

Modern industrial agriculture contributes to climate change in three major ways. First, synthetic fertilizer production is energy intensive and fossil-fueled. Its application releases massive amounts of nitrous oxide (a greenhouse gas more potent than carbon dioxide or methane) into the atmosphere. Regenerative agriculture, described below, is one strategy for overcoming fertilizer dependency. Globally, fertilizers are responsible for an estimated 2.5 percent of greenhouse gas emissions (IFA 2016). Industrial-scale livestock production, second, is also responsible for a copious amount of greenhouse gasses, releasing approximately 37 percent of anthropogenic methane and 65 percent of anthropogenic nitrous oxide (Foer 2019; after carbon dioxide, methane and nitrous oxide are the second and third most prevalent greenhouse gasses). Livestock (especially cattle) are thus a leading cause of climate change. The solution is simple—stop eating so much meat. While a plant-based way of eating may run counter to modern Western diets that are meat-centric, highly-processed, and often-excessive, it offers a simple demand-side solution to climate change that comes with significant health benefits. It is also vitally necessary. If we do not reduce global meat and dairy consumption, we stand no chance of keeping the global mean temperature rise below two degrees Celsius, even in the unlikely event we do everything else right (Foer 2019). Third, wasted food is a significant but often forgotten contributor to climate change. While millions of people experience acute hunger and chronic food insecurity, one-third of food produced is never eaten. As this organic material decays in landfills, it produces large amounts of the potent greenhouse gas methane. Food waste is responsible for roughly 8 percent of total anthropogenic greenhouse gas emissions (Hawken 2017). Solving the problem of food waste will require large-scale systemic solutions, but we can begin addressing this issue at home with proactive waste prevention and composting that puts scraps to good use.

Recognizing industrial food production as inherently unsustainable, a growing number of farmers are developing (or, in some cases, rediscovering) production methods that emulate the complexity of natural systems in order to create food-productive landscapes that can be perpetuated over time. Answering the calls of Wes Jackson (2011) and other leaders of the sustainable agriculture movement, they now see natural ecosystems as models for agricultural ones. Permaculture, for example, refers to "the conscious design and maintenance of agriculturally productive ecosystems which have the diversity, stability, and resilience of natural ecosystems" (Mollison 1988:ix). The emerging field of agroecology similarly applies "ecological concepts and principles to the design of sustainable agricultural systems" and has recently expanded to incorporate cultural, economic, and political concerns (Toledo 2019:86). Regenerative agriculture works to restore degraded land by building fertile soil. This is a major undertaking; today in the United States, topsoil is being lost ten times as quickly as it is replenished and around the world, one-third of agricultural lands are considered degraded. Industrial agricultural practices that strip soil of its organic content—thereby diminishing soil fertility while also contributing to carbon dioxide emissions—are to blame (Montgomery 2017). Degraded soils are unable to support healthy crops without copious quantities of synthetic fertilizers. The result? Contaminated water supplies, algal blooms, and a hypoxic "dead zone" in the Gulf of Mexico covering thousands of square miles (not to mention fertilizers' contribution to climate change). Regenerative agriculture sequesters carbon in the soil, which both improves soil fertility (thereby alleviating food insecurity) and mediates the effects of climate change by offsetting global fossil fuel emissions by as much as 15 percent (Lal 2004).

In the 1970s, Wendell Berry lamented the expansion of modern industrial agriculture, foretelling the decline of farmland and farm culture. "Husbandry will become extractive industry," Berry wrote, and "because maintenance will entirely give way to production, the fertility of the soil will become a limited unrenewable resource like coal or oil" (1977:10). In Berry's view, the tragedy of modern agriculture is rooted in the same exploitative, extractive, expansionist philosophy that underlies most of our social and environmental catastrophes. The debasement of agricultural labor and estrangement of food production from household economies are also to blame. Social dysfunction accompanies ecological destruction, as those who live awash in abundance and leisure remain deeply but inexplicably unhappy. With consumers almost completely alienated from processes of production, wasted water, soil, and energy pass unseen and normalized, while we thoughtlessly swallow "edible food-like substances" (Pollan 2013:5). It is both an ecological crisis and "a crisis of culture" (Berry 1977:38). But it doesn't have to be this way. Even as residents of industrialized regions—where only a tiny fraction of the population participates in food production—struggle to imagine other ways to eat, as much as 80 percent of the world's agricultural yield continues to be generated by millions of small-scale, traditional farmers. Globally, a majority of farmers feed themselves and their families using knowledge and techniques developed over 10,000 years (Toledo 2019:87). It behooves us to respect their autonomy and heed their lessons.

The health and diversity of culture, ecology, and agriculture are mutually interdependent; in case after case, we see that these things flourish—or deteriorate—together. People around the world are sustaining these connections through work in several overlapping movements. The food sovereignty movement—as articulated and enacted by the international group Via Campesina—advocates for the right of all people to healthy and culturally appropriate food that is produced in an ecologically sound and sustainable manner. Perhaps most importantly, food sovereignty implies the ability of individuals and communities to determine their own food and agricultural systems (Escobar 2019). The notion of food autonomy builds on the food sovereignty movement, adding a greater emphasis on peoples' right to make decisions about food that are independent of government or corporate mandates and impositions. Within the United States, the discussion has turned to food justice, which contends that "all communities, regardless of race or income, can have both increased access to healthy food and the power to influence a food system that prioritizes environmental and human needs over agribusiness profits" (Alkon and Agyeman 2011:6). In common with numerous other food movements in the US and Europe, the food justice movement eschews industrial monocultures in favor of small-scale production and fresh, local, chemical-free food. But food justice also draws attention to the reality that "race and class play a central role in organizing the production, distribution, and consumption of food" (Alkon and Agyeman 2011:4). Acknowledging that not everyone can afford to purchase food that is healthy for bodies and ecosystems and that people have disparate personal and cultural food biographies, the food justice movement has become a prominent force in many urban areas.

Because we interact with and think about it so frequently, food is one of the most tangible of all topics. It is also a practical place to start making change, not only because changing our eating habits is so incredibly feasible, but also because such changes turn out to be vitally important tools in the fight against climate change. Project Drawdown ranks reducing food waste and shifting to a plant-based diet as the third and fourth most important things we can do to reduce atmospheric greenhouse gasses (Hawken 2017). Rethinking our relationship with food and restructuring our food system were among the key topics that arose during our initial Next World Conversation. While not all of us have the immediate ability to change what our neighbors eat and how they access their food, each of us is empowered to amend our own eating habits. We can choose food that is as environmentally sustainable and local as possible, avoiding synthetic fertilizers and damaging pesticides. We can reduce our food waste and compost our scraps. And most importantly, we can eat less meat. At an individual level, eating a plant-based diet is one of the most effective actions a person can take to combat climate change; greenhouse emissions could be reduced by as much as 70 percent if everyone adopted a vegan diet or by 63 percent if they adopted a vegetarian one (Hawken 2017). (Those who are not ready to become vegan or vegetarian will be glad to know that every reduction—such as cutting meat from one or two meals each day—helps.) It is true that our individual daily decisions may not amount to much, but the sum of millions of decisions most definitely will (Foer 2019). And there is more. Responding to the enormity of contemporary global problems, Michael Pollan penned a brief essay with the pithy title "Why Bother?" "Planting a garden sounds pretty benign," Pollan writes, "but in fact it's one of the most powerful things an individual can do—to reduce your carbon footprint, sure, but more important, to reduce your sense of dependence and dividedness: to change the cheap-energy mind." (2017:53). Around the world, across the nation, and perhaps even in your community, these changes are already underway.

Our conversation on Local Food and the Future of Agriculture was held on June 25, 2020. Two experts joined us to share their ideas about the food systems of tomorrow. Kip Curtis is an Associate Professor of environmental history at the Ohio State University as well as the director of the Mansfield Microfarm and a member of the OSU Food Innovation Center. Tim Van Meter is an Associate Professor at the Methodist Theological School in Ohio (MTSO) and coordinator of ecological initiatives for the campus, which features a sustainable farm and operates a community supported agriculture network. For this and all subsequent conversations, Terry Hermsen invited the speakers and organized the event, while Anna Willow served as the moderator and host.

☀

Anna Willow: The first thing I want to do is give both of you some time to introduce yourself and the work you've done.

Kip Curtis: I'm working on a food system and community justice project in Mansfield, Ohio. This project began after several years of working in urban agriculture in Florida and thinking a lot about the potential for urban agriculture to serve a justice purpose. When I say urban agriculture, I don't mean the potential to be able to grow food in cities because as long as there have been cities we've been growing food in cities. What I mean is the ability of agriculture to bring not just food but also dollars, business, and income into urban places that are lacking opportunity. So we put together a plan organized around these things we call microfarms. A microfarm is a subunit that is large enough to bring in income, but small enough for an individual farmer or family to be able to work to make that income. So, sort of a family-sized urban plot; about one-third of an acre. The system is designed to succeed in delivering dollars to those places by aggregating growers. So instead of having three or four or five really good urban growers who are competing with each other for the restaurants in town, you get a dozen urban growers who are collaborating to grow the same crop and aggregating at a scale that makes it possible to compete for a local or regional food market. We got the community behind us, support from the university, and a grant from the Foundation for Food and Agricultural Research to pilot this concept over a three-year period. We're at the half-way point right now and, so far, we've been successful.

Anna Willow: Tim, tell us what you've been doing related to food and agriculture.

Tim Van Meter: About ten or eleven years ago, I began to ask questions with our students about how land was being used on our campus. I teach at the Methodist Theological School of Ohio, which has about 90 acres now. The questions turned into what became, about five or six years ago, a campus farm. It started with a little over three or four acres under cultivation the first year. There are now ten acres in cultivation. Currently, we have a 300-share CSA [Community Supported Agriculture]. The farm in some ways is a demonstration, but in other ways it has been a networking opportunity. The farm led to the ability to work a farmers market in Linden, which is a food insecure neighborhood [in Columbus]; it allowed our food to be there and put us in relationship with other folks there. It also helped us develop relationships in the nearby small city of Marion and in other parts of Columbus like Franklinton. And so, we created those partnerships. And also national partnerships. At MTSO we have a strong commitment to being an anti-racist institution and we know that changes in the food system will come with food sovereignty and not just with food security. We work with folks like Reverend Dr. Heber Brown of the Black Church Food Security Network. Questions around food, climate change, and sovereignty for marginalized people are essential to all our questions, so we want to continue pushing those integrated questions.

Anna Willow: One thing that strikes me as I listen to both of you is that food isn't just about food. You might start with food but end up going much farther into other important questions and pressing issues. We have a multidimensional relationship to the things we eat. For the next question, I'll ask you to start us off, Tim. I'd love you to talk a bit about how you envision the next world of food. If you could have it your way, if there were no limitations, what would our food system look like?

Tim Van Meter: With our current economic system, it's impossible. It's related to what Wendell Berry and Wes Jackson have been shouting about for the past 50-plus years. But it requires a whole lot of producers who are doing things on a smaller, organic level. Some of you are familiar with the work of Dr. Rattan Lal. I saw him give a talk about the ability to sequester all of the carbon we've put into the atmosphere since World War II back into the soil just through organic methods, both urban and rural. But that would require moving to farm systems where people are farming ten to 50 acres as opposed to 10,000 to 50,000. And where people have a deep connection to their land. Maybe a farmer of ten acres can feed 300 people. So that would be the vision. It's a collaborative system. There are a lot more people living on the land. Or maybe there are other forms of growing that may not involve human labor but can use organic methods on a much larger scale that are sequestering carbon and building soil. That would be it. You don't build a food system without building resilient soils that can last. Right now, we're strip mining the soil.

Anna Willow: So it's about the soil and ecological processes, but it also sounds like if we're talking about switching from giant megafarms and agribusinesses to much smaller farms, it will also be a major social shift, with a much higher percentage of our population engaged in agriculture, right?

Tim Van Meter: Yes, and it's also asking really important questions about food ethics. Asking "Who will this benefit?" Having a vegan lifestyle that benefits corporate growers and corporate entities does not help the planet. But having a vegetarian/vegan lifestyle that helps the local farmer and helps the people who are putting carbon back into the soils and making a more resilient and robust farming system—that helps the planet. So, in individual consumer decisions, asking "Who will I help?" rather than "What will I eat?" will be an essential part of that.

Anna Willow: Kip, if you could have your dreams come true, what would the food system of the next world look like?

Kip Curtis: That's an interesting question, because I think about what I'm doing more in terms of addressing fundamental social justice questions. But when I think about the food system, I think there are elements that are just absolutely broken, that aren't working. There are elements that are absolutely unsustainable. There is soil mining taking place on a planetary level, with humans moving more earth per day than all of the world's rivers. We're a global force in multiple ways and agriculture plays a significant role. We need to figure out how to reform agriculture. The challenge is that you can't just do that. In the efforts made several times in the 20th century to remake everything from top to bottom through revolutionary change, getting the food system right was usually the first mistake, and it usually led to tens of millions of people dying. So this is not an idle question that we're talking about, both in terms of the genuine ecological and global impacts and in terms of what we do. How do we effect the transformation we need? When I think about that, I think about evaluating what we have. I actually think that there are some agricultural products that have got to be done on scale. When you're talking about grains, you're really better off using some large portion of the Earth that can be dedicated to growing wheat or corn and doing it with global consumption in mind.

…Where I see a lot of really radical transformation is in right-sizing our agriculture. Right-sizing means that while some foods need to be grown on scale, most of the produce section in your supermarket doesn't. Most produce should be grown within 50 miles of where it's consumed. In any urban center, this amounts to hundreds of millions of dollars. You're talking about a robust local and regional economy. I think that shift is underway. It's happening on rooftops in Brooklyn, in fields at MTSO, and on abandoned lots in Mansfield, Ohio. Across the United States, the urban agriculture and local food movement has plotted a new landscape for how we get those kinds of foods. The other section that goes unspoken in all this is the animal side of things. Animals are a tricky question, but I'm a guy who grew up on a sustainable farm where I raised animals that I killed and ate. And that creates a really interesting set of ethical relationships that I have any time I consume meat, which I recognize is an animal—a being—rather than just a slab of nutrition. So, there's a whole new set of ethical relationships, I think, that we've got to embed in the ways we relate to our animals. I think that's happening too.

…I grew up in the 1970s when the sky was falling and we were running out of resources. And some people see what's happening today and say, "See we told you, it's apocalyptic." I don't buy any of that apocalyptic stuff. I think that we, between the 1950s and the 1990s, learned the scope of the problems facing us and from the 1970s onward have been inventing our way out of them. I think we're in the midst of an emergence. Some people are scared of this, but a global system that's rooted in our ability to communicate and our ability to think globally and act locally. And I think that's a real thing that each of our activities contribute to. So when I go up to my microfarm I see the future of farming, when I go to Tim's I see the future of farming. The future is here. We are swimming in it.

Anna Willow: As you were talking, I was reminded of the fact that there's not much difference between the words emergency and emergence. That's something many of us are recognizing right now. For some of us, it feels like the sky is falling, but it's also a chance to lift it back up. Tim, did you want to respond to anything Kip said?

Tim Van Meter: There's a really rich conversation to have around animals and their role in holistic farming. Kip and I would probably be in agreement that eating significantly less meat is a good idea, but within the local farming system we need space for farmers to have animals. And to have what Michael Mercil describes in his artistic work as a *covenantal* relationship.[1] Regarding Kip's point about apocalyptic thinking, theological training gives you a much darker view of the world. Apocalyptic means an in-breaking of a new way of being. So I think it's the possibility of an apocalyptic moment in that a new way of being can break into a time where hope becomes a way when there seems to be no way. And that really is my only hope. I don't think we have much hope in healing systems that are deeply broken, but I wish for that. Because the amount of pain that is possible if systems come completely unraveled is immense. It's not just the socialist movements of the 1940s and 1950s. It's also our dust bowl. It's also the collapse of capitalism at different times in our history. And when the bets become so extreme, there are members of society that get through it okay, but the vast majority of folks who start with limited resources suffer greatly. And that's my fear. But I have apocalyptic hope that something new is in-breaking in the midst of all of this.

Anna Willow: There are clearly challenges. Things are not perfect. And I think we all recognize that. So, Kip, I'm going to ask you first: What do you see as the biggest challenges we need to overcome in order to make some of your positive visions a reality?

Kip Curtis: I like that Tim framed it as apocalyptic hope, because I think more often than not people don't have his sophisticated perspective. We are trained to look at certain things in certain ways. I think a lot of people don't have apocalyptic hope, but they have apocalyptic fear. They're not

---

[1] Mercil's 2012 film on this topic is entitled *Covenant: A Film About Farm Animals (and Us)* (http://www.michaelmercil.com/covenant).

seeing change as something they can engage in in a positive way. And when things are reactive and people carry apocalyptic fear they make poor decisions. They make unwise decisions. They make hurtful and harmful decisions. And so, I think that hope is really important. I walked into the environmental movement with the scientists who were looking at the worst of the worst in the 1980s. And then I went into environmental history and looked at the past in the 1990s and the beginning of the 21st century. I wrote stories of destruction and mining ruining landscapes. And meanwhile, all around me the information revolution transformed the world and created new possibilities for communication. And scientists around the world invented Earth Systems Science, which has created a deeper and more accurate story of humans and life on Earth than we've ever possessed before and projected models of our future with more accuracy than we've ever had before. I think we are in a moment of emergence where our tools are coming together to help us through what is a very threatening time. With the things that we're teaching right now, I have a lot of hope that we are stepping out into this new world that is literally being co-created around us. I think our biggest challenge is pessimism.

Anna Willow: Tim, what do you say to that? What do you see as the biggest challenges we need to overcome?

Tim Van Meter: There's a quote I use from Rebecca Solnit that talks about how darkness can be the darkness of the grave or the darkness of the womb, a dying or a rebirthing. Her book *Hope in the Dark* is one I keep coming back to again and again. I get excited when I'm in conversation with folks like you talking about the possibility of new things emerging. But I also know how hard life is right now for so many people. And so, I think there needs to be a whole lot of the kind of work that Kip is doing happening next. We need to bring in people of all ages who never thought of growing their own food, or never thought they could have some sovereignty or be able to supply their neighbors with food. Particularly in urban areas, but also in some rural areas where there's deep food apartheid. We need to offer a real vision for connection to land that allows people to renew themselves through growing food. Another thing that gives me hope is the idea of respecting our farmers as craftspeople, as artists who bring real knowledge and skills to the land in such a way that deepens the connection. So many folks can tell a farmer what they should be growing or how they should be doing it without having an appreciation of the artistry and craftmanship of that work.

Anna Willow: So those are some of our challenges. I'd also love to hear what you see as the greatest areas of opportunity. What can people like us do?

Tim Van Meter: Since we started the farm at MTSO, we've developed a wonderful network and made this kind of work core to our mission and vision. So what is hopeful or what can be done is to increase the level of connections and the level of work. To find folks who are doing things and help them do it. Connections happen because the right people are talking to each other, because the conversation has broadened so much. People who wouldn't have been in the same room twenty years ago are now having conversations about their shared vision and mission. I mentioned Heber Brown before, who is an important partner because of his national vision. *Food apartheid* is his term, a more honest term than *food desert* or *food insecurity* because it includes the idea of redlining. Supermarkets first come into a neighborhood because they see it as profitable. But they shut down all of the mom-and-pop grocery stores because they can't compete with the larger store. And when the larger store decides their profit margins are no longer high enough, they leave because the economic system allows them to decide this neighborhood has no value. And I think when you make the value judgement to say we will no longer feed these people through the system we created as a corporation, the word apartheid, because of intentionality, is more accurate than desert, which implies that it is a natural system that just kind of grew up without any intentional engagement.

Anna Willow: Bringing the human side of things—which necessarily includes social and political dimensions—into the equation is so central to what we're talking about tonight, so that makes a lot of sense. How do you see urban agriculture meeting the needs of low-income communities in a sustainable way, especially given that local urban agriculture often tends to supply high-end restaurants and is often associated with gentrification?

Kip Curtis: That's actually the most scathing critique of urban agriculture, and it's coming from social scientists of color who are seeing a kind of colonialism and a whole lot of structures replicating themselves. Detroit is the poster child for urban agriculture turning into gentrification. And it's a very serious problem. I think understanding the dynamics of the problems that we're facing today is really critical. And I think Tim is right; food desert is too soft a word because it makes it seem like it was an accident. And particularly when it comes to race, it's *not* an accident. When it comes to job loss, it's *not* an accident. There are a series of decisions embedded in that. But the value of food is a complicating factor. Supermarkets don't leave because they don't care; supermarkets leave because they're not making a profit. So we have a very serious problem of food distribution, and there's a very serious need to get food to the hungry. We have created a system of wealth and social mobility with a historical record of marginalizing very specific groups of people. The landscapes that have resulted have been landscapes with no capital, no opportunity. This is poverty we're talking about. And food deserts are a measure of household poverty. And, as the term food apartheid highlights, racism as well. Where those two things overlap, we have a crisis that has haunted this country forever.

Tim Van Meter: Communities gathering together to keep the dollars circulating in the community is really essential, so local growers, local distribution, local wash-and-packs, small local markets are really important. Our urban communities and our rural communities have been strip-mined for wealth. Wealth leaves those communities and goes into corporate coffers, into the hands of very few. So it really is a kind of removal of wealth from the people who create it. If we can help urban growers and rural growers who are abused or dismissed from the system and allow them to maintain their own wealth from their own production, and to circulate it among their neighbors, I think that's vital.

Anna Willow: So true! We have great questions from members of our audience, so I'd like you to have a chance to address some of them. Going forward, what do you see as the role of technology in the future of agriculture? On the one hand, we can't help innovating and wanting to do things more efficiently, but on the other, technology is also harming the climate and ultimately ourselves. How much technology is the right amount?[2]

Kip Curtis: I'm a historian of technology. Historians are not supposed to be prognosticators, so I could get everything wrong. That said, I think part of the matrix of emergence is technology. I have shifted over the course of my career from being anti-technology to realizing that if you are anti-technology you leave all of the design questions to people you don't like. I'd rather have those design questions in the hands of people who share my values. We designed the microfarm project with a value in mind: We want to make the farmer absolutely necessary, but we also want to make him productive. I'm working with some engineers right now on building Smart Beds to automate some of the extremely time-consuming tasks like reading nutrients and irrigation. Don't remove the farmer; make his job a higher-level thinking job. I think that's the balance that we're after here. We live in a hybrid world. We live in a world of nature and culture. We live in a world of organics and technology. And those things do not have to be in conflict with one another, although they often are, and they do raise challenges for us. I'm an optimist.

Tim Van Meter: Technology is never just neutral. Those of us who use technology—which is every breathing human being—make decisions about the values that we will bring to that technology. So I am all for agricultural technology that increases the value of the farmer, the value of the food produced, and the value of the soil. When we're talking about agricultural technology, anything you can do for an agricultural product that increases its value is positive for the farmer. And so, I think we need to lose the delusion that all technology is bad or wrong. We're never going to stop using it. And we have to claim its value.

Anna Willow: One last question. How can we kickstart the implementation of the local food system when people from disadvantaged communities are increasingly seeing and naming capitalism as a greed-centered system? How can we kickstart what you've talked about given the inequities and constraints we face?

---

[2] We would like to thank Ingrid Wood for posing this question.

Tim Van Meter: You saved the easy one for last.

Anna Willow: First thoughts at least?

Tim Van Meter: The Linden neighborhood in Columbus is a really interesting place because you have about six different churches or community organizations who aren't cooperating well but are all doing really interesting work. Personally, I think it would be significantly better if they could cooperate, but also within that space, they're beginning to align resources in multiple ways with local communities. And that is really helpful. All of them are leveraging resources into a neighborhood to try and make a significant difference. And the larger that web of cooperation grows, the better the use of those resources. The other thing is identifying who's doing what and then learning enough about them to find out if they're talking to each other. And if they aren't talking to each other try to find out why. And then align yourself with the people who seem to be doing the best work. That's my start.

Kip Curtis: The microfarm project is my answer to that question. You figure out how to create robust local partnerships, you put together an extension training program, you develop a cooperative, and you get a charitable investment to get it kickstarted. And it takes two or three years to get it off the ground. We've learned an enormous amount in Mansfield. A long-term goal—and by long-term I mean five to ten years—is that this will not be something that we go after charitable dollars for, but instead will be something municipalities pass bonds to invest in. There are millions of dollars in food consumption that leave every single small city in America. There is a tremendous opportunity to channel food dollars that are already being spent in the economy into the households and neighborhoods that need them most. And it's simply about tapping that flow with a system that can do that sufficiently. It's not rocket science. I wouldn't be able to do it if it were rocket science. So we're kickstarting now. I've been at it now for four years in Mansfield. We have witnessed greater successes that I ever could have imagined. We are forging the future there. I am convinced of it more and more each day.

The food systems of the future will involve transitioning away from industrial agriculture and the current system we have today. It will mean focusing on growing locally, growing organic, and growing things that can actually feed people rather than just corn and other cash crops used for nutritionless food.
~George, 11th Grade

4

The Next World of Energy: Peril and Promise

As leading environmental authors have argued, we are entering a period of major transition for humanity and for every species on this planet (Orr 2009:3; Wahl 2016:15; Hawken 2017:x). As Naomi Klein states bluntly, "we need to be very clear: because of our decades of collective denial, no gradual, incremental options are now available to us." She goes on to quote climatologist James Hansen, who remarks, "in the face of an absolutely unprecedented emergency, society has no choice but to take dramatic action to avert a collapse of civilization. Either we will change our ways and build an entirely new kind of global society, or they will be changed for us" (Klein 2014:23). With greenhouse gas emissions driving potentially catastrophic climate change, energy use is at the heart of our current crisis. So much of the contemporary world of business, industry, transportation, housing, and daily life depends on energy use, which up to this point has implied the large-scale extraction of fossil fuels. Still, as with the rest of the climate crisis, these problems mean that there is also great opportunity. Our crisis is a chance to create new jobs and new infrastructure via renewables and to shift our patterns of consumption. As such, ours is a time of immense peril and much promise—*if* we can transform our culture in time.

Peril #1

As we foster the next world of energy, perhaps the biggest peril is our reliance on fossil fuels. Let's acknowledge the basic facts. Although "global energy-related carbon emissions fell by 5.8 percent in 2020, or nearly 2 gigatonnes of carbon dioxide, thanks to reduced demand for oil, coal and gas…the International Energy Agency predicts that energy-related carbon-dioxide emissions will rise by 1.5 gigatonnes to 33 gigatonnes in 2021, an increase of almost 5%" (The Economist 2021).

The largest contributions come from three sources—China, the European Union, and the United States, which produce 41.5 percent of global greenhouse gas emissions—while the bottom 100 countries produce only 3.6 percent (Friedrich et al. 2020).

The sheer magnitude of the numbers above and in the chart below reflect our reliance on these "cheap" sources of energy. Their prominence in nearly every facet of American life places energy at the center of the central problem of global climate change. Of course, when all of the externalities are accounted for, fossil fuels aren't cheap at all; even in the short-term their costs in environmental damage and health impacts are immense. And then there are the immeasurable costs that rising temperatures, rising seas, and extreme weather will bring. There are many ways to estimate the amount of greenhouse gasses (GHGs) emitted by various sectors of the US economy. The US Environmental Protection Agency's breakdown of GHG emissions by sector in the year 2019 is shown below (based on USEPA no date):

Greenhouse Gas Emissions by Sector

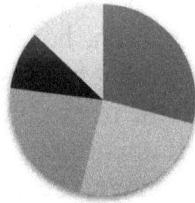

■ Transportation ▨ Electricity ■ Industry ■ Agriculture ▨ Commercial and Residential

You will notice that nearly every piece of the pie (with the possible exception of agriculture) relies on energy use to sustain itself. Let's consider the four largest sectors in a bit more detail. Transportation (29 percent of 2019 greenhouse gas emissions) generates the largest share of greenhouse gas emissions. Greenhouse gas emissions from transportation come primarily from burning fossil fuels to power our cars, trucks, ships, trains, and planes. Over 90 percent of the fuel used for transportation is petroleum based, which includes gasoline and diesel. Electricity production (25 percent of 2019 greenhouse gas emissions) generates the second largest share of greenhouse gas emissions. Approximately 62 percent of our electricity comes from burning fossil fuels, mostly coal and natural gas. Industry (23 percent of 2019 greenhouse gas emissions) produces greenhouse gas emissions from the burning of fossil fuels for energy, as well as from chemical reactions necessary to produce goods from raw materials. And finally, the commercial and residential (13 percent of 2019 greenhouse gas emissions) emissions arise primarily from fossil fuels burned for heat, the use of products that contain greenhouse gasses, and the handling of waste (US Environmental Protection Agency no date).

Truly absorbing the numbers on this chart should make us shiver, for it requires no special expertise to recognize the vast quantity of greenhouse gasses released when we burn fossil fuels to power these economic sectors. Couple those staggering numbers with this one from Paul Hawken, focused on the national and international monetary support for fossil-fueled production. One impediment to decarbonization, Hawken writes "is inequitable government subsidies. The International Monetary Fund estimates that the fossil fuel industry received more than $5.3 trillion in direct and indirect subsidies in 2015, that is $10 million a minute" (Hawken 2017:3). Whatever we align to secure the purchase of renewable energy, in Ohio or elsewhere, stands before such massive fossil fuel support like David before Goliath.

Promise #1

In our whirlwind of hope and despair—the human tendency to say, "surely we can overcome any problem," while simultaneously doubting our efficacy—we often find ourselves returning to Paul Hawken's stunning compendium of climate solutions published in *Drawdown: The Most Comprehensive Plan Ever Proposed to Reverse Global Warming*. He phrases our hopes well in the closing paragraph of his introduction:

> [Our situation] can tempt us to believe that global warming is something that is happening to us—that we are victims of a fate that was determined by actions that

precede us. If we change the perception, and consider that global warming for us—an atmospheric transformation that inspires is to change and reimagine everything we do—we begin to live in a different world. We take 100 percent responsibility and stop blaming others. We see global warming not as an inevitability but as an invitation to build, innovate, and effect change, a pathway that awakens creativity, compassion, and genius. This is not a liberal agenda, or is it a conservative one. This is the human agenda (Hawken 2017:xi).

Hawken's words percolate hope, backed up by solution after solution. His book is full of work already being done around the world, with details and metrics that prove that change is possible. For example, onshore and offshore wind turbines are ranked #2 and #22 on Hawken's list of 100 ways to reduce atmospheric carbon dioxide. His team claims that "in the United States, the wind energy potential of just three states—Kansas, North Dakota, and Texas—would be sufficient to meet electricity demand from coast to coast" (Hawken 2017:3). The development of regional microgrids is also full of promise. Microgrids would allow a wide range of households, companies, and governments to produce their own energy and sell it to the grid. From there, it would be distributed amongst their constituencies, with little or no waste, in contrast to "burning coal to boil water [where] two-thirds of the energy is dispersed as waste heat and in-line losses" (Hawken 2017:5). Geothermal energy is another exciting possibility. Ranked by Hawken's team as #18 in overall benefits (despite some issues with chemicals released in the process), "39 countries could supply 100 percent of their electricity needs from geothermal energy" (Hawken 2017:7).

There are many more examples, but you get the idea. Technical solutions to at least some of our problems lay before us, given the political and economic will. Combine the above with Solar Farms (#8), and Rooftop Solar (#10)—which entail introducing small solar installations in places around the world which have hitherto lacked access to electricity in any form—and we begin to feel that we might surmount our challenges after all.

Further Perils

Such optimism for a more regenerative approach to energy aside, neither Hawken nor anyone else would pretend that our path will be smooth. Without going into great detail on our other, deeper challenges, let's list a few problems that will take years—if not decades—to overcome:

❖ *The deep inequities built into our energy system.* In an article entitled, "Where the Poor Spend More Than 10 Percent of their Income on Energy" and subtitled, "Hint: Almost Everywhere in the United States," Adam Chandler quotes DeAndrea Newman Salvador, an economist and founder of The Renewable Energy Transition Initiative. "Lower-income households fall into something we and others call "energy poverty," which is when someone spends just under about 10 percent of their income on energy-related expenses," Salvador says, "Compare that to a middle-to-upper income that may spend 5 percent or less" (quoted in Chandler 2016). In some regions, low-income families can spend greater than 20 percent on their income on energy. Such statistics correlate with the emphasis that drives much of the conversation to follow and will be a major impediment to any regenerative energy future.

❖ *The capacity for "dark money" to undermine our efforts* (Mayer 2016). There are powerful political forces seeking to thwart attempts to shift to renewables, reduce waste, and decarbonize our energy systems. To view one of the most glaring examples of such behind-the-scenes maneuvering, we need look no further than Ohio's House Bill 6 scandal. As summarized in the *Dayton Daily News*, House Bill 6 sits at the center of a public corruption case. Former Ohio House speaker Larry Householder was arrested on July 21, 2020. Householder and four other men were charged with racketeering. Prosecutors allege that an unnamed company funneled more than $60 million in bribes to Generation Now and other dark money groups. The money was used to elect pro-Householder Republicans to the Ohio House so that Householder could return as House speaker. In turn, Householder helped pass House Bill 6 and defend it from a referendum attempt in the fall of 2019. A nonprofit funded by Columbus-based American Electric Power gave $900,000 over three years to two groups that don't have to disclose their donors. IRS documents show that the nonprofit Empowering Ohio's Economy Inc. donated $550,000 in 2019, $50,000 in 2018 and $100,000 in 2017 to Generation Now, which federal prosecutors allege was the primary vehicle for funneling bribes to former Ohio House Speaker Larry Householder (Bischoff 2020). Much more could be said about this case, which is still being processed in the legislature and the courts, but for now, let it simply illustrate the difficulty of making long-term energy changes when so much money can be put into play on the side of the fossil fuel industry.

❖ *Our deeply entrenched habits.* One additional peril will serve to illustrate how hard it will be to reduce the profligate energy use that permeates American culture. We could look at our heavy reliance on air-conditioning or the copious waste generated by building construction, but let's instead consider the deeply-entrenched lawn-care industry and its multi-billion dollar commitment to keeping nature pruned back via the small-scale internal combustion machinery known as lawnmowers, leaf-blowers, edgers, and their ilk. In a 10-minute round of "lightning research," a recent class of mine found a number of troubling statistics. The following is a telling sample of what they discovered:

> "Dr. Chuanhui Gu, a professor in the geology department at the Appalachian State University [found that] a 2.47-acre plot of lawn in Nashville, Tennessee, produces greenhouse gases equivalent to up to 2,443 kg of CO_2 per year. This is equivalent to the amount produced by a flight more than halfway around the world. Dr. Gu also states that standard lawns emit about 5 or 6 times more CO_2 than what is absorbed during photosynthesis. Nitrous oxide emissions from fertilizers lead to an estimated total equivalent of about 25 million tons of CO_2 each year in the US. Gu adds that if clippings were left to decompose on lawns, the US could store up to 16.7 teragrams [16,700,000 tons] of carbon each year in the soil" (Hitchler 2018).

In addition, the class found that one gas powered lawn mower emits 89 pounds of carbon dioxide and 34 pounds of pollutants per year, as much as eight new vehicles driving 55 mph for the same period of time. Using a lawn mower for one hour has the same carbon footprint as a 100-mile car trip (Lawson 2006). According to the EPA, mowing lawns produces a huge amount of carbon dioxide, contributing five percent of the total US greenhouse gas emissions (Jonas 2020).

While such statistics are alarming, even more ominous is our deeply-ingrained psychological attachment to our freshly-mown lawns (Robbins 2007), as habitual as popping into our cars many times a day for individual trips to the store, school, work, and sporting events, lawn-mowing is a habit we need to unlearn. It is vital that we alter our energy-use patterns, reduce our emissions, and change how decide what we need and why.

Further Promises

In closing, let us consider two examples of programs, developments, and concepts that foreshadow the promise of a fossil-free future. First, in the conclusion to her co-edited volume, *Energy Democracy: Advancing Equity in Clean Energy Solutions*, Denise Fairchild (featured in Chapter 5 for her transformative economic ideas) gathers numerous examples of communities simultaneously addressing climate justice and transitioning to renewable energy. In the District of Columbia, for instance, there has been a large shift in that direction, with the District government installing solar on 130 low-income homes between 2013 and 2015. Furthermore, Fairchild notes, "in July of 2016, activists successfully passed legislation to create a Solar for All program, which increased DC's investment in low-income solar from $1 million to more than $20 million annually" (Fairchild 2017:224-225). Many additional examples within the volume show how people working at the ground level have been able to make significant advances, often overcoming the impediments put in place by fossil fuel companies and their lobbyists.

Second, in a trend noted across the country during the COVID-19 pandemic, many individuals, companies, and communities have found that lessening the amount of time spent commuting to work (which has added benefits of reducing traffic and vehicle emissions) could become a long-term trend. A *New York Times* article by Matthew Haag, entitled "How New Yorkers Want to Change the Streetscape for Good," conveys this unfolding vision:

> Of all the ways the pandemic reshaped New York City's streetscape, the most profound example might have been found on Vanderbilt Avenue as it cut through brownstone Brooklyn. On weekends jazz bands played on the corners. Friends reunited on the median. Children zigged and zagged on their bikes as diners sat on bistro tables atop asphalt…in what became an organic takeover and reimagining of the city's streets across its five boroughs (Haag 2020).

Couple that with statistics showing how even a small drop in the number of people on the roads during rush hour could reduce greenhouse gas emissions (Badger 2021) and we may find that the slowdown of our driving habits during the pandemic gives us reason for hope—if these trends can lead to long-term changes of habits and desires. Are we willing to make these changes in our lives? Are we willing to move toward the world we want? Only time will tell.

We were joined on August 20, 2020 by Randi Leppla (an environmental lawyer who at the time served as lead energy counsel for the Ohio Environmental Council) and Jon-Paul d'Aversa (then the senior energy planner at the Mid-Ohio Regional Planning Commission) to talk about the future of energy. As d'Aversa suggests in the conversation that follows, we need to replace fossil fuels, but that is not all we need to do. Along with embracing renewable energy, might we call for and create a world where we need energy less? Might we shift from a *car culture*, where the bulk of our decisions, policies, and habits are driven by the "cheap energy mind" (Hawken 2017:53) and the almighty automobile, to a *caring culture*, where our jobs, our mindsets, and our daily lives revolve around sustaining basic needs, supporting each other, and restoring the health of humanity and all species on the planet? Could we call such a culture shift the biggest promise of all?

Anna Willow: Welcome! The topic of this evening's conversation is the next world of energy and we're going to be thinking together about how we can create the energy sources and systems that will support a sustainable and resilient future. So let's talk. Jon-Paul, can you tell us about the work you've done to bring cleaner and greener energy to central Ohio communities? Why is this work so important right now?

Jon-Paul d'Aversa: There are tons of things we could talk about. I've been with MORPC [the Mid-Ohio Regional Planning Commission] for about three years, and it's been non-stop the whole time. To start with, the Franklin County Energy Study was a big undertaking. It is a compendium of energy consumption, emissions, and expenditures across the whole county. But one really important piece of it was our energy burden metric. We analyzed every zip code to find the percentage of income that goes towards heating, cooling, and electricity. And that became the basis for a lot of other work in Columbus. It was the basis for the application for the American Cities Climate Challenge that Columbus won and for a lot of work with the utility companies. I think one of the most important things that came out of the energy study is that it laid the groundwork for long overdue conversations about equity and race. Since we had the data behind the things everyone was talking about, we were able to jump right in and advocate for the communities. Connected to this, MORPC has really given me a platform to discuss how our country has a policy of poverty and how the struggles that our communities face are woven into the fabric of our built environment. And so, I've been talking a lot recently about how policies of the early 1900s—things like redlining, the federal housing authority, and also the GI bill—led directly to higher energy consumption in in poorer areas. And that leads directly into the health impacts of poverty situations that a lot of these communities are facing. So that's been hugely important, and we've been making connections with people who are in positions to actually effect some change. Just to round things out, in 2021 MORPC has a lot of cool new programing coming out. We have the Clean Energy Acceleration Program, which is moving our local government to 100 percent clean energy. And there is also our Clean Mobility Transitions; we're going to jump in and see what we can do to revamp transportation and move towards an emission free system.

Anna Willow: So, it sounds like issues of equity and access can't be separated from the clean and green part of my question. That's something really important that's been coming up again and again in our Next World Conversations, so thank you for sharing that. I'd love to hear from you now, Randi. What kind of work have you been doing to bring cleaner and greener—and more equitable—energy to central Ohio communities? Why is your work important right here and right now?

Randi Leppla: This work has always been important for those of us who are in this fight. But we are obviously on a very short timeline now. We know that we have about ten years to do something if we hope to avoid the worst impacts of climate change. To return to Jon-Paul's point about equity, those impacts will hit our environmental justice and frontline communities first and worst. And so, in everything we do we are working toward a cleaner energy future. We have to not just take into account, but actually *include* frontline communities in the planning and decision-making, because we can't sit back and assume we know what's best for those communities. We need to include them in the conversation. And, you know, OEC [the Ohio Environmental Council] is no different than any other environmental organization. We've all got a lot of work to do as far as race and equality are concerned. The environmental movement has historically been a white-led movement and we've left a lot of people behind. So that's something we're being really intentional about right now. We've been working closely with the city of Columbus on the aggregation program they're rolling out. Historically, aggregation has been a tool for folks to bundle their energy together and save money, but we can also bundle our energy together demand cleaner renewables, local renewables, and solar development nearby so that our air quality improves. Another piece I'm really excited about is Power a Clean Future Ohio, which is a non-partisan coalition. We did a lot of soul searching as a coalition to figure out how we could make this work. There are a lot of programs that aim to achieve a certain percentage of renewables by a certain year and those are really important, but we didn't want to leave any community behind. So we're tailoring programming to make sure we are getting everybody involved, because we need everybody in this fight. We have programs tailored around four areas: increasing renewables, increasing energy efficiency, working on electrification to reduce carbon emission, and carbon capture, which includes carbon sinks through green spaces. We've got several communities that are already signed on, so I'm really excited about that. Those are just a couple of examples.

Anna Willow: Both of you have a lot going on and it sounds like really important work. Randi, I'd like to have you continue and think a little bit more about some of the visions that you, your organization, and others that you work with have for the future of energy. If you could have it your way—if there were no limitations, no nasty politics standing in your way—what would our energy systems look like?

Randi Leppla: Right now, the House Bill 6 scandal is the backdrop for pretty much everything I'm doing. But beyond that, we have lots of ideas about what a better energy future looks like for Ohio. Number one, we would lean into energy efficiency. The cheapest and cleanest kilowatt hour is the one that we're not using, the one we're not producing. Thinking about what things will look like on the other side of the pandemic, there are over 85,000 jobs in efficiency in the state of Ohio, and those cannot be outsourced. If we are weatherizing our homes, we are putting people back to work. We're also reducing costs for folks who have been hit hard by the pandemic or lost jobs. The second obvious thing to be doing is rapidly shifting away from fossil fuel. I can't stress enough how necessary it is to reduce our CO_2 emissions. And another thing we would like to see is more distributed energy. Right now in Ohio we aren't able to do true community solar. We need a legislative fix to allow virtual net metering so we can all take part in clean energy in the state.

Anna Willow: Jon-Paul, your turn. If you could have it your way—if things were working well—what would our energy system look like here in central Ohio?

Jon-Paul d'Aversa: I'll piggyback in a moment on what Randi was saying. But right before this conversation I was reading an article saying how we need to move from a fossil fuel dependent energy system to one that's dependent on renewable energy. And it struck me, because I started thinking: "Why are we dependent on energy at all?" Now, what exactly this energy independence system looks like I don't know yet. But I think that would be a really good question to consider. Aside from that, the last thing Randi said about decentralized energy generation is huge. You might have heard it referred to as Grid 2.0. It's basically the utility serving as the marketplace. So rather than the utility being the entity providing the system by which we get electricity, we're selling any energy we can generate onsite at our house or our business into this marketplace. Think of a farmers market; that's what this new version of the utility looks like.

...Another super important thing that we tend to forget about is the transportation network. This is one of our largest sources of greenhouse gasses. And thus far, we've been prioritizing cars. This is very unique to the US. We prioritize individual forms of transportation, which makes it very apparent that we don't view transportation as a human right. Somehow, it's okay to expect people to have to get to work so they can pay taxes, so they can get benefits, but we're not providing them with a way to get to work. We're actually making it *more* difficult by prioritizing cars, which are the most expensive and the most polluting form of transportation. If we continue to focus on a car-centered transportation network we will always be leaving people behind. We'll never reach that point of equity. The last thing I want to bring up wasn't originally my idea but I thought it was really cool. A gentleman I was speaking with at a conference a few years ago in New Orleans was asked, "If you could do anything what would it be?" And he said, "I would allow doctors to prescribe energy efficiency." It's brilliant because we know the health impacts and cite them. Physically and also mentally, the stress of paying energy bills is such a burden to people that if we can approach this from a public health perspective—like we now are with racism—we might actually be able to make some pretty impressive headway.

Anna Willow: These questions about why we depend on energy at all, where that dependence comes from, what it means for us as human beings, and how we shift our culture away from this kind of dependence are really interesting. The idea you mentioned of prescribing energy efficiency would imply a major cultural, societal, and systemic shift. These are the kind of things that keep me up at night, so it's exciting to see that people with different perspectives are thinking about these questions as well. Jon-Paul, I'd like you to keep going with this next question. What I'm wondering is where you see evidence of this next world of energy actually working. Could you give an example or two of where things are going well?

Jon-Paul d'Aversa: Absolutely. We're seeing a lot of Grid 2.0 being built out in different countries. Africa (specifically, Nigeria, Uganda, and Tanzania) and India have been really big on this. They're test beds for solar and microgrids, which are more or less the central components needed to make it happen. We're not only seeing that these systems are more resilient, but also that people have a better ability to bounce back from adverse situations or to avoid some of them entirely. As far as the transportation system goes, basically any country is doing better than the US when it comes to prioritizing mass transit. It's going to take a cultural shift on our part.

Anna Willow: Your turn, Randi. Where do you see things working well? Are there examples and models either from close to home or from farther away that we can look to?

Randi Leppla: Although I have a negative outlook right now because of House Bill 6, not everything in Ohio is bad. There are some really exciting things happening right here in our backyard. Solar United Neighbors of Ohio is a co-op that gathers homeowners together to sign up. They are doing some incredible work and the number of systems installed is growing by the day. We've had to get politicians out of the way because Ohioans have made it very clear that they want this, and it is not based on party lines. They want to choose where their energy comes from and they understand the value of it. In addition to household installations, we're also seeing large companies demanding solar as well as wind. So I think that that's really a bright spot. There's so much going on with solar both at the rooftop level for individuals and utility-scale, if we could get the legislature to give us virtual net metering so we can do community solar and make sure that everybody's able to take part in this shift that would be really wonderful, but there is already a lot of movement right now.

Anna Willow: You've talked a bit, Randi, about some of the challenges we face, not only House Bill 6, but also other legislative challenges. Do you see that as the biggest challenge we need to overcome in order to realize a positive energy future? Or are there other challenges that come to mind?

Randi Leppla: Yeah. I think gerrymandering is a huge problem. We have representatives who are in such safe districts that they think they don't have to listen. And like I said, an overwhelming majority of Ohioans want more renewables. They like energy efficiency; they like saving money. So I think that's an important thing to overcome, because if we don't have politicians in office who are listening, we end up with artificial barriers to the things that make the most sense. Hopefully we can overcome some of those challenges, have a level playing field, and elect leaders who will listen to us.

Anna Willow: Jon-Paul, what about you? What do you see as the biggest challenges we need to overcome in order to make our visions a reality?

Jon-Paul d'Aversa: I'm glad Randi spoke about the legislative side of that, because I want to take the other angle. I know some people disagree with this perspective, but I think the biggest barriers we face are personal. Even some of the most outspoken, green people we know are still driving cars. And they're still buying meat, and so on down the line. So in January, I gave up my car. Fortunately, I live downtown so I am able to walk the two miles to work and the two miles back. I wanted to see if I could do it, because I needed to be doing my part. And what I found was that I love walking. I love riding my bike. I love seeing the city wake up in the morning on my way in. I love meeting my neighbors. I love talking to the homeless people that I see out there all the time. It's really been nothing shy of poetic. But nonetheless, I went into it scared. I was worried that I wouldn't be able to hack it and I told myself I would give it a couple of weeks and if it doesn't work out, I would just buy a new car. But it has been a really wonderful experience for me.

...I think there are a lot of ways we can take on climate change ourselves, whether it's small things like eating less meat or switching our lightbulbs or giving up our cars or just riding our bikes more. There are so many opportunities we can take advantage of. Now, I'm in a position where I can do these things and a lot of people aren't. So that's another piece that I think is hugely important and brings the discussion back to equity. I think it's essential that we tackle equity, and I think our current inequitable system is one of our biggest barriers to real change. I keep thinking about how many people could actually be allies in the fight against climate change but can't because they're worried about how they're going to pay their bills. Or how many more resources we could devote to this fight but can't because they need to be directed to something else just so people can get by. Or how much brainpower we could have in this fight if we hadn't excluded so many people from experiences and employment opportunities. I think if we take the time to build an equitable society, we'll be in a much better position to tackle climate change.

Anna Willow: So, Jon-Paul, you've already been talking a lot about areas of opportunity. There are challenges, of course, but there are also opportunities to change our personal behavior. I'm curious about what you see as our greatest opportunity. What can people like us do to help put pieces of our next world into place? What can we do tomorrow, next month, and next year?

Jon-Paul d'Aversa: I'm glad Randi mentioned Solar United Neighbors. For those who aren't familiar with solar co-ops, essentially it means getting as many people in your community together as possible so you can purchase solar panels at the cheapest price and have everybody put them on their house. It's a great model. You know what I want to see? I want to see that happen with energy efficiency. We don't even need to wait for someone to come in and start a program. Talk to your neighbors. Pick up a contractor pack of LED lightbulbs or new filters for your HVAC units. Go around to each other's homes and make sure in the summer they have a removable UV tint on the windows. Make sure the windows are covered with plastic if they're drafty in the winter. We have an opportunity to make this not just something we do one time, but to make it an annual tradition. Heck, let's make it a holiday! Doing this would strengthen our communities and open up opportunities to help each other and become resilient in every way. So, I think capitalizing on our ability to build community and taking the energy efficiency approach is our best opportunity right now.

Anna Willow: That's an amazing idea. Again, we see efficiency, community, and equity going hand in hand rather than working at cross-purposes. Randi, I want you to have a chance to answer the same question. What can local people like us do to put pieces of the next world of energy into place? What can we start doing right now?

Randi Leppla: One thing I encourage everybody to do is get involved at the Public Utilities Commission and the Power Siting Board when projects you care about come up. There are opportunities to speak up and speak out about this stuff. I think sometimes people don't know where to start, but if you are interested in getting involved, we will take you. It's an open-door policy. The one last thing I'll say is to make sure you vote, because that will help us in the long run.

Jon-Paul d'Aversa: For anyone interested in getting involved, the number one most important thing is just to show up. You don't have to be embarrassed. I have found family in the sustainability field here in central Ohio. I will totally greet anyone with open arms because I love to see people getting into this work.

Anna Willow: I often find myself thinking about what the world will be like 20 or 30 years from now. And I find myself wondering about scale. Is personal, self-sufficient energy generation a realistic thing to strive for? Should we be striving for microgrids with small-scale generation projects? Or is the future going to be a future of macro-grids more akin to what we have right now but with renewable sources of energy generation?

Randi Leppla: I think for the efficiency of the grid, you will want your power sources as close to you as possible, because every time electricity has to travel through powerlines we lose a lot of efficiency. So, a distributed grid makes the most sense. It's possible to have large scale solar projects, but wind farms are by definition a little more distributed. It only makes sense to have a more distributed system. The very large systems, like what we have for today's coal plants, should be a thing of the past because they're polluting and also because they're just not as efficient as they could be if the power sources were closer to home.

Jon-Paul d-Aversa: I agree. I think in the future producing electricity where you are using it will make the most sense no matter which sustainability or resilience metric you decide to apply. I also think it's important to remember that there is no one-size-fits-all solution. What works in Columbus may not work in Cleveland or anywhere else. So we will need to come at this through many different angles and be open to a bunch of different solutions.

One of the big things for me in the next world will be having a clean, renewable source of energy. When we look at all the issues that come from unclean energy sources, it's starting to affect the way we are able to do things on Earth. One of the big things will be finding ways to stop relying on finite resources and looking for cleaner ways.
~John, 10th Grade

5

An Economy That Works For Everyone

Imagine the economy as an iceberg, with only wage labor and capitalist market production occupying the small visible tip. Filling the much larger area below the surface are myriad diverse activities—ranging from caregiving and volunteer work to informal lending and barter—that are typically excluded from economic discourse and overlooked as powerful economic drivers. In *Take Back the Economy*, economic geographers J.K. Gibson-Graham, Jenny Cameron, and Stephen Healy use this memorable analogy to underscore the fact that the economy is far broader and more amenable to our influence than we are taught to believe.

Our society's collective refusal to see below the surface represents just one of many disempowering and destructive economic assumptions. Most of us learn that the economy operates like a machine, guided by a proverbial invisible hand. Somewhere along the way, we come to accept that the only way "regular" people like ourselves participate is by directing our income to the purchase of goods and services. We see the economy as larger than ourselves and outside of our control. But when we expand the frame to incorporate informal and unpaid economic activities, it becomes clear not only that we play important economic roles but also that we have the power to help our communities prosper. By redefining the economy broadly to denote how people collectively organize themselves within a society to create material wellbeing, we open up a broad vista of alternative economies that have long been neglected by conventional coverage (Johanisova and Vinkelhoferova 2019). Turning again to the iceberg, we find that "once we include what is hidden below the waterline—and possibly keeping us afloat as a society—we expand our prospects for taking back the economy" (Gibson-Graham et al. 2013:11).

In addition to citizens' alleged inability to influence the economy in non-consumptive ways, we have been told that economic growth is inherently good. Whether the scale is personal or national (or somewhere in between), we are told that bigger is better, that excess equals success. Consuming conspicuously is, in fact, how many people measure their own worth against that of their neighbors. But once basic needs are met, economic growth does little to improve quality of life. In the United States, the economy has grown exponentially since the 1950s (with a temporary dip during the 2008-2009 recession and a steeper "V" associated with the COVID-19 pandemic), yet self-reported happiness has been on the decline since the 1990s (Helliwell 2019).[3] Economic inequality has also risen sharply in recent decades; while the rich keep getting richer, the middle classes shrink and the poor struggle to survive (Horowitz et al. 2020).

Clearly, growth does not promote human welfare. And it certainly does not promote environmental quality or sustainability. Since the industrial revolution, the economic growth doctrine has contributed to environmental decline, with natural resource extraction and energy-intensive, polluting forms of production constantly expanding and accelerating to meet newly invented needs (Willow 2018). Traditionally, Gross Domestic Product (GDP) has been the standard metric of economic health. Problematically, however, GDP measures national spending and market transactions while ignoring their environmental and social causes and consequences. For this reason, alternative measures—the Genuine Progress Indicator and Gross National Happiness Index are foremost among them—that reflect the holistic wellbeing of people and planet are gaining traction (Costanza et al. 2014). As noted by our Next World Conversation guests, these alternative measures encourage us to imagine an economic system in which quality of life counts.

Recognizing the reality produced by business-as-usual as profoundly unjust and unsustainable, growing numbers of academics, activists, and social leaders are calling for a transformation in both how we think

---

[3] Happiness declined even further in 2020 as a result of the pandemic and associated isolation (see https://worldhappiness.report/).

about the economy and how the economy operates. We need an ethical economy, guided by morality, responsibility, and community. In stark contrast with the current system, this new economy will be "a space of decision making where we recognize and negotiate our interdependence with other humans, other species, and our environment" (Gibson-Graham et al. 2013:xix).

Proposals for economic transformation have taken various forms, all which attempt to reconcile economic, environmental, and social goals (D'Amato et al. 2017). Green and circular economies do this by reforming existing systems of production, distribution, and consumption to augment their sustainability. A green economy, according to the United Nations Environment Programme, is one that improves human wellbeing and builds social equity while reducing environmental risks and scarcities.[4] Expanding from this loose definition, green economic visions incorporate sustainable investment, efficient resource use, increased recycling of materials, low-carbon production, and job creation in ways that overlap with key UN Sustainable Development Goals. While noble in its intentions, the green economy idea has been critiqued for its relatively conservative stance and its unwillingness to question dominant economic assumptions. Lamentably, the green economy remains focused on the imperative of economic growth, suggesting that it is firmly ensconced within dominant capitalist economic paradigms (Brand and Lang 2019). Advocates of a circular economy attempt to redesign production systems to use as few new materials and produce as little waste as possible. With increased recyclability and regenerative products, the circular economy eschews the planned obsolescence that plagues and perpetuates today's "throw-away" society (D'Alisa 2019). Used colloquially to denote an economy in which nothing is squandered, circular economies have the potential to promote social justice. Still, most work in this area has yet to substantively incorporate such concerns and, like the green economy more broadly, the concept has been critiqued in some circles for its uncritical acceptance of economic growth.

---

[4] https://www.unenvironment.org/explore-topics/green-economy/about-green-economy (accessed February 2, 2021).

In recent years, advocates of a Green New Deal (also discussed in chapter 9) have voiced many of the most vehement calls for economic transformation. Demanding dramatic, comprehensive action akin to that seen during the 1930s response to the Great Depression, proponents argue that our political goals must reflect the urgent reality of our situation. Climate science tells us there is no time to waste if we hope to evade the most catastrophic effects of global climate change. While there does not exist any single codified Green New Deal program, climate leaders agree that gradual action is no longer sufficient. "An *effective* Green New Deal," argue Aronoff et al. "is also a *radical* Green New Deal" (2019:18). Most Green New Deal proposals concur on the necessity of keeping the vast majority of known fossil fuel reserves in the ground, instituting a carbon tax to disincentivize fossil fuel use and provide revenue to fund green programs, eliminating fossil fuel subsidies, developing a renewable power grid, incentivizing renewable energy production and storage, promoting electric vehicles and their requisite infrastructure, building and retrofitting low-and-no emissions structures, planting carbon-sequestering forests, reducing agricultural dependency on petrochemicals, and providing green jobs workforce training (Aronoff et al. 2019; Klein 2019; Rifkin 2019). Because substantial government spending is required to realize these grand ideals, political will is a necessary ingredient—and so far a major impediment—to achieving a Green New Deal. Still, there is reason for hope. Polling in the US and beyond indicates widespread public support for such programs across the political spectrum. And investors and businesses have already begun shifting toward renewable energy as major economic sectors decouple from fossil fuels (Rifkin 2019). Justice within and between regions is recognized as a vital component of the Green New Deal. Because the wealthy industrialized nations are largely to blame for the climate crisis and possess the resources necessary to address it, it is widely acknowledged that they should be responsible for financing a global Green New Deal. As Noam Chomsky suggests, the goal of achieving net zero emissions by 2050 must be met "in a way that also expands decent job opportunities and raises mass living standards for working people and the poor throughout the world" (Chomsky et al. 2020:74).

Green New Deal proponents recognize that change is inevitable. "There is a growing sense that we are paying a terrible price for the fossil fuel civilization that we built and exulted for more than two centuries," economic theorist Jeremy Rifkin observes, but "a younger generation is coming forward with an intimate sense of the darkness that is unfolding around them and a steely determination to break through the lethargy that has allowed us to slip to the very edge of a planetary crisis" (2019:46). We know our economic system cannot continue in its current form. It operates only in the short-term and benefits only the very few. Decarbonizing our atmosphere and our economy is the most essential undertaking of our time (and perhaps of *all* time), but it must proceed fairly if it is to be socially as well as environmentally sustainable. Too many discussions about post-carbon economies celebrate cold quantifications and technological fixes, while ignoring issues of equity (Heffron and McCauley 2018:74). But increasingly, we are coming to understand environmental destruction and social injustice as tightly intertwined. The economy sits at the intersection of physical and human realms, operating where biogeophysical degradation (or renewal) and social despair (or security) meet. While industry propaganda often pits jobs against the environment, this is a false dichotomy. We need an economy that works for everyone, a "just transition" that ensures safe, sustainable, and fulfilling work for all who seek it (Henry et al. 2020; Morena et al. 2020).

Held on October 22, 2020, our Next World Conversation about building the economies of the future reminded us that our current economic system is not the only option. There are, in fact, countless alternatives to late-stage capitalism's destructive, depersonalized status quo. Around the world, diverse alternative economic arrangements already exist in both surviving traditional and new experimental forms; fair-trade markets, self-provisioning, in-kind exchange, and caregiving labor are just some of the possibilities (Gibson-Graham 2008:616). Complementary currencies are one striking example of how local people can create strong and sustainable local economies. Discussed in detail during our conversation, complementary currencies are "forms of money created by non-state actors as alternatives to and remedies for the perceived pathologies of state-created money and growth-focused development" (North 2019:92). While such currencies take a variety of forms, they are almost always created by people who seek to strengthen local control over economic life. They promote positive resistance and resilience and provide a way to keep money—and power—in local hands (North 2014:253).

Our conversation revealed that we are far from powerless, that individuals and communities have the capacity to take economic matters into their own hands in order to "create worlds that are socially and environmentally just" (Gibson-Graham et al. 2013:xiii). We were joined by two inspiring experts. Denise Fairchild directs a national nonprofit organization called the Emerald Cities Collaborative, which works to create sustainable, just, and inclusive local economies.[5] Fadhel Kaboub is an Associate Professor of economics at Denison University who conducts research on sustainable prosperity. Together, we considered how we can take steps toward an economic system that supports a healthy planet, provides fulfilling new jobs, and addresses deep social inequities.

☀

Anna Willow: Both of you have done really important work to envision and create more sustainable and equitable economies, which is why we invited you to join us tonight. For people who aren't yet familiar with your work, could you tell us briefly about some of your key projects, goals, and signature visions?

Denise Fairchild: I'm glad to be part of this conversation about the next world economy. I'm the National Director of Emerald Cities Collaborative. My work is born out of a 40-year history of organizing, planning, and environmental and economic justice work. Emerald Cities, for me, represents my capstone project in which all of that comes together. Emerald Cities was founded about ten years ago, when we were in the last economic malaise and the economy was in the toilet. The founders of Emerald Cities started thinking about how we could reimagine and rebuild our economy. It seemed that for the first time in a long time, people were in the same boat—and that boat was sinking. And so, they brought together labor, community organizations, youth

---

[5] To learn more about Emerald Cities Collaborative, visit https://emeraldcities.org.

organizations, policy advocates, and think tank people to figure out how to build a three-part vision. How do we green our cities? How do we do it in a way that is economically just? And how do we do it in a way that is democratic? In other language, it might be called the triple bottom-line: Environment, economy, and equity. And that work is done in coalition. How do we dismantle the barriers to such an economy? How do we make sure there is a shared language, a shared vision, and a strategy to get us there? Community groups can organize, but if we're not engaging corporations, the environmental community, and the government we're only dealing with some of the challenges that need to be addressed. So we've been doing this work for many years. The whole idea was to harness public, corporate, and institutional investments around green infrastructure development. We focus on greening the built environment to address the issue of sustainability, but also make certain we're rebuilding the middle class and ultimately ensuring that low-income people of color who have been left out of every other mainstream economy—whether agricultural, industrial, suburban, or digital—are front and center not just as consumers but as producers. Most of our work has focused on the energy sector—energy efficiency, clean energy, and distributive energy systems—but we've also been building local sustainable food economies and clean water infrastructure. We can build on that going forward.

Anna Willow: I can't wait to hear more! Fadhel, could you tell us about some of the work you've done?

Fadhel Kaboub: Thank you for having me; it's wonderful to meet so many new friends. In my academic work, I was initially motivated by questions related to unemployment, poverty, economic justice, and social justice. I wasn't really into the environment until about ten years ago when it became very clear to me that the clock is ticking. We have ten years to act on a massive scale. So I started using everything I have in my toolbox as a progressive economist to think about how we can bring about bold, transformative solutions. And everywhere I turned in the progressive community and the environmental movement, the same question eventually came up: "How do you pay for it?" That happens to be the area I've been working in for a long time. I belong to a school of thought called Modern Monetary Theory (MMT for short), which has tremendous implications for the kind of work we're trying to do. Can we actually afford these massive transformative solutions? Things like a Green New Deal, Medicare for all, reparations? Where does the money come from?

Anna Willow: What does MMT say about that?

Fadhel Kaboub: The basic MMT insight is that the federal government of the United States, like most sovereign governments, has the capacity to issue its own currency. We've been told by mainstream economics that government spending is limited by tax revenues and borrowing capacity. So we can tax and spend, and borrow a bit if we wanna spend a bit further. But beyond that, we enter a slippery slope to hyperinflation and printing too much money. Everybody is familiar with this story. You don't have to be an economist to believe it. MMT says that limit is actually much higher, that a country like the US can spend much more than what we're currently spending. The last ten years since the 2008 economic crisis is a case in point. Although there has been a massive amount of quantitative easing by the Federal Reserve, huge deficits, and a rising national debt, there isn't even a hint of the inflation measures that economists and central bankers fear.

…From an MMT perspective there are two things that determine the risk of inflation. Number one is the shortage of productive capacity. In other words, if we run out of skilled people, engineering capacity, and materials, prices will start going up. Dealing with productive capacity is a wonderful thing because it allows us to plan strategically for areas of the economy where we lack capacity in health, education, infrastructure, and green energy. And we build more. And we create more. And we innovate. Number two is where I think our troubles lie. According to MMT, the second risk of inflation is when you have areas of the economy with too much market power and market concentration, where key players can raise prices and cause inflation simply because they can. Because they have too much power. And that kind of inflation is not going to go away by implementing austerity and spending less. You only get rid of that risk of inflation by taxing and regulating their market power out of existence. In other words, you democratize those industries. We're talking about big oil and gas, big pharma, Wall Street, health insurance companies. We all know who they are and we all suffer the consequences because they raise insurance premiums and there's nothing we can do about it. They raise monthly internet fees and there's nothing we can do about it. Because there's no competition.

...If we're going to tackle the climate crisis, we're going to need to spend big right now on bold, transformative policies. But if we don't push that risk of inflation out by increasing our spending capacity, we won't be able to do it. So what is standing in the way? Productive capacity, we can deal with. We can produce more, we can innovate, we can train people. But for big corporations that hijack the economy and raise prices simply because they can, we need to tax and regulate their power out of existence. Who's going to do that? We have 535 people that we usually call lawmakers. They make the laws. Their job is to regulate the economy. And if we have a true democracy, a government of the people, by the people, for the people, then the problem is solved. But if we have a government of the Super PACs [Political Action Committees], by the Super PACs, for the Super PACs—which is what we have right now—then we're in trouble. We won't be able to make the changes we need in time to save our children and grandchildren unless we tackle this obstacle. That's the framework I work within. I recognize the political constraints. I recognize the challenges. We can't win this fight unless we mobilize, educate, organize, and empower people to know what the possibilities are. I believe a better future is within reach. People need to know what the possibilities are and believe in the possibilities, but also be well-informed about the constraints and who's standing in the way. Otherwise we will end up running around in circles and not knowing where to go. And we just can't afford that.

Denise Fairchild: I appreciate that approach. But another thing we do at Emerald Cities is follow the money that is being spent. The world we live in now and the economy we have today is how global capital behaves. And it doesn't behave well or decently. It is an extractive economy. The question is: How do we harness the money that is currently being spent to behave differently? We are looking specifically at current expenditures from corporations and the public sector and utilities. How can we harness those expenditures to build sustainable, just, and inclusive societies? For example, many of us in the environmental justice community don't like cap and trade, but it still raises billions of dollars. In California alone, utilities spend $1.4 billion each year on energy efficiency projects through cap and trade mechanisms. The question is, then, spending on what and how? Are we spending this money in ways that are anti-racist and anti-sexist? Are we spending it in ways that are going to be universally accessible? I believe we have the ability to transform markets, and I absolutely agree that a monopolistic economy is tainting not only our economy but our politics as well. So how do we dismantle monopolies and global capital in a way that creates decentralized networks, locally owned and controlled economies? We can ask the public sector and government to come in and regulate, but I think through the power of organizing we can get the capital that is currently spent to behave as a solidarity or moral economy.

…Let me give you two quick examples. We're working with health institutions that have committed to offering 100 percent sustainable food in their patient meals. We created a community benefits agreement not only to bring sustainable food into areas that need it, but also to hire from the community. So we'll be hiring 250 individuals as we develop this new system and buy from Black and Brown urban farmers within a 250-mile foodshed. We're bringing food into a new sustainable model. Think about COVID-19 and what it did to our food economy: Our food economy collapsed. We had farmers dumping milk in the Midwest because they couldn't get it to the consumer markets while people in the consumer markets were standing in lines because they couldn't get to the food. So how do we shorten our supply chain and create products and commodities locally? How do we change our economy to be local, sustainable, and inclusive? We are also working with major tech companies. Many of them are making commitments to use 100 percent renewable energy by 2025 or 2030. By themselves, tech companies buy two gigawatts of power per year. How do we harness that purchasing power to buy and build local community energy cooperatives and create jobs and business opportunities? I think that capital is there without necessarily having to tax people. You can play on people's corporate social responsibility, whatever sensibilities you want to engage to use capital in a more productive way. That's building a different kind of economy that works for everyone.

Fadhel Kaboub: Absolutely. Most of my work as a macroeconomist is in the MMT space and the Green New Deal national program, but as I said earlier, I'm a realist and I don't expect 535 members of congress to change course anytime soon. So of course we have to work at the local level. We can mobilize local resources without having to wait for the federal government to do the right thing; we can help new local economies thrive. One approach is the creation of local community currencies. Community currencies have been around for hundreds of years and they tend to thrive during really bad economic times. In communities in the US and around the world, these currencies began popping up left and right after the covid crisis started. They tend to be designed to support small, independent business and to keep business in town. And they tend to be relatively small scale, rather than at the scale we're talking about when we talk about creating jobs and bringing social justice and equality. It's simply about retaining as much business as possible. If I live in a small town and earn my income from the university in that town, but I go to the big city next door to spend my money on the weekend, that is an example of money leaking out of the community. That's a huge problem many small communities struggle with. Community currencies keep money in town.

…With those experiences in mind, we decided to design a larger scale complementary currency, one that can keep its value stable (at one-to-one with the US dollar) and can be a huge source of job creation at the local level. We designed three anchors to keep the currency stable. The first is community owned and managed credit card processing that takes the transaction fees that usually go to Wall Street firms and reinvests them in the community instead. If you imagine a mid-sized city, that amounts to hundreds of millions of dollars. Although those are US dollars rather than a complementary currency, that becomes the anchor. In town, now you can create a local currency that you can use for local purchases. And if you want to buy something from outside the area, you can buy it with the US dollars you generate through this payment system. So this first anchor gives everyone in the community—especially the merchants—an incentive to use the community owned and managed credit card processing company because it's bringing revenue to the community. And now the community can design a program to spend and invest in the most neglected areas of its economy.

So what you have is an incentive structure that can jumpstart job creation and community development and create green space within an economy that cares for people, the planet, the elderly, and children in a transformative way. Another part of this is to give merchants a bonus when they use local currency, for example, on a $100 transaction they might receive $90 in US dollars and $15 in local currency. They will say, "Great, but how do I spend the local currency?" So we are building a network of businesses and community partners who are collectively agreeing to use the local currency. This brings us to the second anchor, which is the ability to pay utility bills and city taxes in local currency. Imagine your city saying, "As a partner in this community development program, we agree to let you pay your city taxes, your sales taxes, your property taxes, and your fines and fees in this local currency." That second anchor guarantees that anybody who earns local currency can, at a minimum, pay their taxes to the city. Now the supermarket is willing to accept payment in local currency because they pay sales, property, and corporate taxes to the city. And merchants can pass the bonus points they get from using local currency along to their customers in the form of discounts. With local dollars come discounts, so you incentivize their use for merchants and customers. Finally, the third anchor of our complementary currency is the role of community banks that guarantee that it stays one-to-one with the US dollar. This is accomplished through a market incentive (such as when a consumer pays a transaction fee to purchase local currency from the bank so they can receive local discounts) and a regulatory incentive (in this case, the Community Reinvestment Act allows banks to qualify for credits for community development work).

…Notice that through all of this, we didn't have to raise taxes, borrow from anybody, or ask the federal government to send us grants. This is local people with local capabilities mobilizing resources to demonstrate that we can build homes, renovate, employ people, and pay them decent wages without having to wait for the federal government to wake up and create the Green New Deal. With this program, you can create a local Green New Deal where you build productive capacity and renewable energy. There are plenty of possibilities. What it takes for a program like this to launch is mobilizing people to come together and say, "We're all in."

Anna Willow: Denise, I would love to hear what synergies you see between Fadhel's ideas about complementary currencies and the on-the-ground work that you and your organization have been doing.

Denise Fairchild: We work within the context of the circular economy. We take our current economic system sector by sector and disaggregate by aggregating up. What do I mean by that? In the work we do—whether it's the food sector, energy sector, or transportation sector—we are aggregating the demand for products and services. It's not just to create jobs, but really to dismantle the centralized, monopolistic, toxic sectors of the economy. Decentralize the toxic food sector, decentralize toxic energy. How do we dismantle the centralized grids, sector by sector, and create decentralized economies that allow us to create a circular economy? It's not just about the number of jobs or businesses you create. We're taking the investments that are currently being made in these sectors of the economy and transforming entire systems to behave differently. So major food companies, all of a sudden, are out of business because no one is buying their food. Food buyers are now saying, "I want a different framework. I want to buy local. I want 100 percent sustainable. I want union wages. And I want benefits and opportunities for the areas I serve." Institutions are now seeing synergies between health, wealth, and climate resilience. Their mission, more and more, is embedded in the wellbeing of a community and they are looking at communities in a holistic way, seeing how the environment and the economy impact health.

...Spending money in a way that creates locally owned, locally controlled economies is important, but I think the bigger question is this: How do we live large on less? It's one thing to have everybody get a piece of the pie, but if the pie is poisoned, then why are we eating it? If it's an extractive economy and we cannot harness it to behave differently, then we have to build something completely new. We in America are 5 percent of the population, but we're taking 23 percent of the globe's holding capacity. We are taking God's gifts to us, our natural resources. We have a model of mass production, mass consumption, and mass accumulation of wealth. How do we rethink an economic paradigm that rebalances our economy with our ecology? That has to be the larger frame of the vision I have for an economy in the new world that we're creating. That it is sustainable. That it is not measuring wealth on the basis of Gross Domestic Product. That we're using measures such as the wellness or happiness index that recognize that it's not about wealth, but rather about the richness of our lives, the richness of our relationships, and the richness of how we relate to our environment. How do you use what we call *the time value of money* in your community, whether you use local currency or barter with your neighbors? How do you use the fact that I do childcare and the fact that you fix cars as a form of exchange in the community? It's about creating the kind of community economies that have historically supported African American communities and so many others. In the days of slavery, African Americans had to survive through collective economies, and we continue to grow in this space. We're seeing energy co-ops and food co-ops and the slow food movement. The seeding of cooperative local economies is happening everywhere, and I think it's coming from consumers' appetite for something different, something local, something healthier, something greener. But we're also driving the demand and aggregating the capital that's already being spent, investing it differently and shifting markets so they behave differently.

Anna Willow: I have two last questions I'd like both of you to address. What do you see as the biggest challenges we need to overcome in order to make these positive economic visions a reality? And what are the areas of opportunity? What can people like us do to put pieces of this next world into place?

Denise Fairchild: I think the biggest challenge is Western cultural values. We *want* stuff. We are mass consumers, whether it's because we actually need all of this or because it's being pushed on us by corporations. Increasingly, I'm taking my frame from the context of the environment and the ticking clock, so I think we have to realign what our civilization needs and come to terms with the challenges of corporate capitalism. We need to think about what it's doing to our spirits, our communities, and our economy. We're not getting any messaging that speaks to living large on less. Most people are still talking about climate change in terms of renewable energy, but this doesn't shift our economic framework away from the mass accumulation of wealth and consumption and exploitation. No one is speaking about the fact that it is not sustainable. We cannot continue to live like this. So I think our cultural values are the biggest thing in the way. And what we can do individually is to check ourselves. At the local level, it's about how we organize ourselves. We have a lot of power as consumers that can be used to change how capital operates in our communities and we don't use it. Instead of using corporations to work for our communities, we are being used. We can change our individual behavior, but I think that through collective power we can also make major transformations as well.

Anna Willow: Fadhel, what are the biggest challenges we need to overcome? And where do you see opportunities for people like us?

Fadhel Kaboub: There are plenty of challenges, but also plenty of opportunities that go unnoticed. I'll start with the opportunities, because that is where our action matters. There are many things we can be doing as individuals, as communities, and as a nation to decarbonize and reduce our energy consumption. It has to do with investing in local sustainable food and local microgrid infrastructure that is more resilient. We have to push back against the standard narrative that says, "No, no, no! We can't do that because we need the fracking jobs." People think we need the corporate power because that's how we fund our schools and how we create jobs. But it turns out that isn't true. A group of colleagues and I have been producing a monthly green jobs report and it looks like greener jobs are more resilient. Greener jobs pay better. Not only are greener jobs more resilient during a crisis, but they also they recover faster as we exit the crisis. Green jobs are the jobs of the future, so we need to invest in that direction.

…And to amplify what Denise said earlier about changing the metric, if we're going to change the paradigm, we have to change the metric. Our obsession with economic growth is literally killing us. What is included in the metric of economic growth? Every time a water source is polluted and people have to undergo cancer treatment, GDP goes up. Economic growth is created when people get sick, because they pay hospital and medical bills. All of that is celebrated. But our quality of life is diminished. Some ecological economists have produced an alternative metric that takes the GDP number everybody celebrates and strips it of the negative elements that reduce our quality of life. Every time we build a prison GDP goes up. Every time there's a war GDP goes up. Every time we pay interest and penalties to Wall Street banks, GDP goes up. But none of that improves our quality of life. While GDP has been growing for the last 40 years, the Genuine Progress Indicator (or GPI) has been flat. Once they see that GDP has been going up but quality of life has been flat, most citizens say they are interested in quality of life improvement. They ask, "What are the investments that will increase our quality of life?" And it's all of the things that we've been talking about. Sustainable food. Public health. Education. Green energy. Clean water, clean air, clean soil. So there is a huge consensus. There are so many possibilities for mobilizing people at the local and national level. But it requires a paradigm shift. It requires looking at the standard picture and tilting your head sideways and saying, "I see it differently." There is a whole world of possibilities here. This is what we're struggling with as a nation, as a global community. How do we make that paradigm shift? How do we bring people together? Public opinion surveys show that green jobs, the Green New Deal, clean air, clean water, clean soil are massively popular ideas for Republicans, Democrats, and Independents alike. Nobody hates clean air, right? But what do people hear from the political system, the establishment, and the media? They hear, "If you want to invest in green jobs instead of coal and oil and gas, your job will be on the line. Your community will starve for money." This is our opportunity to call their bluff and say that a better world is within reach. We have the resources to do it. We have the skills, talents, opportunities. And to be honest, we have no other choice. Sooner or later it will happen. We just need to do it now, when it is not too late for the next generation.

Anna Willow: So many of us are taught to focus on money. Realizing that we can assess things differently is really important. We can look at our jobs differently. We can look at the quality of our lives differently. But how do we change our values so that we no longer bow down to the dollar? How do we actually shift our collective focus so we can elevate these next world economic systems on a large scale?

Denise Fairchild: This is happening already. You see it at your local farmers market. The number of folks who believe in the value of our environment and our natural world is growing. Climate change is forcing us to think differently about how we're living our lives and whether we're going to have a life worth living. We are thinking now about how we build resilience. We're being forced to think about our lifestyles, our economy, our supply sources, and our financial capital as well as our social capital when we encounter any disaster. That is the new normal. We don't have to look for the new normal. We are already in it, with constant disasters of one sort or another. All of the research suggests that the number one thing that gets people through a challenging time is how they relate to each other. And we can expand that to think about how we relate to capital and how we relate to our environment. Whether we want it or not, those changes are being foisted upon us. The question is how do we make these changes at a scale and in a timeframe that allows us to address the urgency of the moment?

Fadhel Kaboub: What we're talking about is raising public consciousness. And that requires popular education and engaging people in conversations that present the possibilities, the opportunities. You can be angry at the system, but lack any vision of what's possible, because you've been told "This is it." Like Margaret Thatcher once said, "There is no alternative." That's what we've been told, right? You can be angry at inequality, socioeconomic exclusion, and the climate crisis. And maybe you can even see some of the possibilities, but you still say, "It's too expensive, it's unaffordable; we need to stick to the current extractive system because it supplies cheap food and cheap energy." We push back, but they convince us again with that narrative. We need to empower people with a counter narrative that supports a paradigm shift. Education is key. Textbooks have taught generations of young people that there's nothing they can do. And coalitions of politicians, lobbyists, and media companies spin their stories to reinforce the same status quo. We have to push on all fronts—at the federal, local, and community levels—so that people have a counter narrative and are mobilized and well informed.

*Local currencies will have to be part of our new
world. They focus on one of the
main things that will be part of creating this
world: Working together as a community.
We have to implement that in all aspects. I think
implementing a local currency can start to bring
us back down to earth, to more communal and
sustainable economies.*

~George, 11th Grade

6
Education and Engagement

For the vast majority of human history, children learned most of what they needed to know through observation, experience, and play (Gray 2013). Stories shared by elders provided additional instruction, along with entertainment and a common cosmology. Much of life transpired outdoors and interaction with nature was constant. And because education was inseparable from everyday life it, too, was grounded in connection to diverse non-human communities.

Fast forward to the 2020s. Kids are much more likely to be found attached to an electronic gaming device than outside. They rise before the sun, pass the day in one or more classrooms, and return home to complete homework, attend scheduled extracurriculars, and (if time permits) consume as much screentime as their parents permit. How did it come to this? The omnipresence of limitless distractions is part of the problem, but not all of it. In many neighborhoods, scant opportunities exist for children to roam legally and safely, while allowing them to do so is widely perceived as tantamount to neglect. Many adults now see unstructured outdoor play, once a staple of childhood, as both dangerous and unproductive (Louv 2005). Eventually, children are unable to even imagine what they might do outside and on their own.

While opportunities and outcomes vary widely, rigorous academics that fill them with facts, competitive sports and assorted lessons, and abundant playthings aren't making most young people happy. On the contrary, the number of children experiencing mental illness is unprecedented. One in six children in the US between the ages of six and seventeen has been diagnosed with a mental health disorder like depression, anxiety, or attention deficit/hyperactivity (ADHD). Only half of them obtain treatment (Whitney and Peterson 2019). Rates of suicide among young people are equally devastating, increasing by almost 60 percent between 2007 and 2018. In some regions, suicide is now the leading cause of death for adolescents and teens (Curtin 2020). The COVID-19 pandemic has exacerbated these troubling trends.

While the solution is clearly more complex than mandating time outside, interaction with the natural world does seem to be an important part of the equation. For children, nature appears to be a potent therapy for the treatment of ADHD and other disorders (Louv 2005). Adults experience comparable results; increasingly, we recognize that some form of environmental connection is essential for our mental and emotional wellbeing (Roszak 2001). We are drawn to nature, and we thrive in its proximity (Wilson 1984; Williams 2016). Spectacular vistas and remote wilderness, as valuable as they are, are not required for people to benefit from natural immersion. Experiencing and celebrating nearby nature—the wildness in our own backyards—is essential if we hope to develop a responsible and realistic environmental ethic (Cronon 1995). The irony, environmental writer Richard Louv explains, is that even as we realize how much our wellbeing depends on nature, the amount of time young people spend in natural settings continues to decline. Louv coined the term *nature deficit disorder* to describe this broken bond. Reducing the deficit is essential, Louv declares, because "our mental, physical, and spiritual health depends upon it," and because "the health of the earth is at stake as well" (2005:3).

We need nature. And, we now know, nature needs us. We need scientific research that illuminates complex couplings of human and global biogeophysical systems. We need environmental science education that elucidates these relationships, so that regular citizens can comprehend that what befalls the Earth also befalls us, its sons and daughters (as the quote commonly attributed to Chief Seattle goes). But at least as important as knowledge, we also need to feel. We need a sense of place, a connection to the Earth—or at least some small portion of it—to convince us that the world is worth caring for (Chapin et al. 2011). As the renowned biologist Stephen J. Gould once proclaimed, "we will not fight to save what we do not love" (1994:40). Numerous outdoor education programs have built on the realization that caring about something makes people much more likely to protect it and are actively nurturing place attachment and positive affect as a way to foster pro-environmental behavior (Kudryavtsev et al. 2012). Ideally, ecological awareness and connection can—and should—also happen organically, through everyday experiences. Chasing fireflies. Counting birds. Planting seeds.

Not only are standard upbringing/schooling strategies failing to create children and adults who are ready and able to care for the environment, but they are also failing to help learners reach their full potential (Gray 2013). These are not new problems. Eighty years ago, John Dewey advocated for an intimate relationship between education and "actual experience" (Dewey 1986 [1938]:244). Rather than imposing standards, subjects, and methods selected by adults on hapless young minds, he argued that young people should learn through free activity, individual expression, and experiences in the here-and-now world. Taking inspiration from a different pedagogical tradition, Indigenous educator Gregory Cajete's conclusion is similar. Cajete (Tewa) sees the crisis of American education as rooted in modern identity and disconnection from the natural world. At its essence, he suggests, education entails "learning about life through participation and relationship in community, including not only people, but plants, animals, and the whole of Nature" (Cajete 1994:26). When we share knowledge in the context of day-to-day life experience, we reclaim learning as a creative and ongoing act.

While still the exception rather than the rule, the number of institutions acknowledging the value of experiential learning continues to grow steadily. Preschools, parents, universities, and even public school districts (as the conversation you are about to read demonstrates) increasingly admit that education is at its best when it expands beyond the classroom and encompasses direct encounters with its subjects (Kolb 2015). Consider just a few of the possibilities:

❖ In the realm of preschool education, the Regio Emilia model has gained a following for its lack of set curriculum. Initially developed with post-WWII rebuilding funds in the Italian town of the same name, Regio Emilia schools are based on the belief that young children are capable of initiating their own learning. Rather than directing what children learn and when, children are able to pursue their own interests. Teachers facilitate and guide students' experiences and explorations, which often occur in outdoor settings (Hobson 2020).

❖ The unschooling movement offers an alternative for parents and students who are dissatisfied with conventional education. Situated at the unstructured end of the contemporary homeschooling spectrum, unschooling allows children to learn through everyday life experiences rather than following a set curriculum. Students select experiences based on their own interests, strengths, and learning styles. As unschooling expert Gina Riley (2020) sees it, unschoolers gain intrinsic motivation, autonomy, and a sense of relatedness (most often to their families, but outdoor versions of unschooling promote an analogous sense of relatedness to the natural world).

❖ Whether conducted within or outside of school settings, Youth Participatory Action Research (YPAR) affords adolescents and young adults the opportunity to investigate issues that affect their lives and empowers them to take action in response. Through YPAR, students "learn how to study problems and find solutions to them" (Cammarota and Fine 2008:6). Not only do young people gain skills that complement their knowledge, but they also gain equally vital confidence in their capacity to analyze problems, conduct research, and take action. YPAR helps young people imagine that change is possible; as they come to understand problems' causes and consequences, they stop accepting their inevitability. As such, this mode of experiential learning can be an important force for change.

❖ School gardens adorn an increasing number of preschools and elementary schools. Gardens promote connections across curricular areas, integrating science with history, literature, and the arts, while instilling a deep understanding of cultural landscapes (Zarger 2008). Above and beyond their formal educational value, gardens are rare places where kids (and teachers) experience joy, healing, comfort, self-expression, and healthy relationships to other people and the environment. After conducting long-term participatory ethnography in a school garden in Michigan, Laurie Thorp emerged convinced that "if there is any hope for reinvigorating our system of science education…it will be found not by increased teacher accountability, not with more rigorous scientific curricula, but rather through our sense of wonder" (2006:47). In a public education system that evaluates success based on standardized test scores and little else, gardens offer a welcome respite both to teachers struggling to promote students' holistic learning and personal development and to students struggling to link learning to life.

These are but a handful of real, replicable ways that education can connect young people to the natural world while simultaneously nurturing their imaginations and empowering them to strive for a fulfilling future.

Why are imagination and empowerment so important? Eric Liu and Scott Noppe-Brandon define imagination as "the capacity to conceive of what is not…the ability to conjure new realities and possibilities" (2009:19). Imagination, in other words, gives us the ability to dream, envision, and create. Confronting the conjoined catastrophes of climate change, ecological decline, and social injustice will require innovation and self-efficacy. If we hope not merely to survive, but thrive, in the decades ahead, we need to do things very differently. The road to radical change begins with the belief that another world—one different and better than the dystopian nightmares offered by popular futurescapes—is possible. And we need to trust in our capacity to make the positive worlds we imagine real. According to Liu and Noppe-Brandon, the socioecological crises we now face are not failures of willpower, as is so often assumed; they are instead "failures of imagination" (2009:7). Our conventional education system is partially to blame.

For generations, our schools have excelled at teaching helplessness and acceptance. Whether accidentally or by design, conventional education eradicates rather than cultivates creativity, constricting our personal and collective conception of the possible (Hopkins 2019). In school, we learn content and routine. We learn to do what we are told. But it turns out that critical, creative thinkers *don't* always obey. Imagination poses a serious threat to the status quo neoliberal doctrine that implores us to believe "there is no alternative." Instead of learning to ask questions, we are trained from an early age to normalize unsatisfactory circumstances. Upsetting encounters and incongruous expectations are "just the way it is." But for the health of our souls and our society, we need to overcome these habits, to dream and to do. We need to believe that the next world is ours to create, that today's problems can be solved in wonderful ways.

We were joined on November 18, 2020 to discuss how experiential environmental education can meet the needs of today's young people—who will soon be tomorrow's adults. The conversation was steered by the story of the Granville Land Lab, a conservation project initiated by students in 2013.[6] While recognizing that a significant amount of education occurs outside of school settings, we are confident that this conversation captures the challenges and opportunities that large numbers of contemporary educators and learners face. Two experts showed us what is possible. Jim Reding is an ecology and environmental science teacher at Granville High School (located in Granville, Ohio). He was named the North American Association for Environmental Education's 2016 Educator of the Year. Dustin Braden is a recent graduate of Ohio Wesleyan University and Jim Reding's former student. He played a major role in the Land Lab's creation.

Anna Willow: Our ultimate goal is to envision together what a bright future for our communities and our world can look like. One logical place to begin is with our children and the schools they attend. Jim, can you start us off by telling us about some of the amazing things that have been going on at Granville High School?

Jim Reding: Thanks; it's nice to be here tonight. Just to give you a little background, my environmental science students are challenged with what's called a "take action" project. Rather than just talking about environmental issues, they have to come up with solutions—things they can engage in, things they can do, and things they can change about the world around them, whether it's locally or nationally. One particular

---

[6] To learn about the Granville Land Lab, see https://thelandlab.wordpress.com/who-we-are/.

class I had around seven years ago decided that one of the things they wanted to do was to create an environment that could connect students to the natural world. They saw this lack of connection as one of the limitations their generation faced, so they came up with the idea of creating a Land Lab. One of the things that always amazes me when we do these projects is how much students are actually capable of when they get an idea and take off on it. They do amazing, impressive things. It's incredibly inspiring to watch.

Anna Willow: How did the Land Lab take shape?

Jim Reding: Seven years ago, there were 43 acres of corn and bean fields next to Granville Intermediate School. That's where the students decided to do their work. As part of these projects, they typically have to come up with funding. They enlisted the help of several people, including Brent Sodergren from the US Fish and Wildlife Service, to come out and go over their plan. Based on their conversation with Brent, they ended up taking on a much grander challenge. From an original plan to work with four or five acres, we ultimately ended up with a Land Lab covering over 40 acres. What was once corn and bean fields is now prairies, forest complexes, wetlands, and vernal pools. It's a thriving ecosystem. In a matter of two years, we were seeing diversity there that we didn't even expect to see. To get to that point, we enlisted many partners. The students had a chance to work with many different organizations and groups of people. They had a really authentic experience, sitting across the table from professionals in jobs they might ultimately want to have. Today, we have around 100 acres of Land Lab with nine different habitats. We've planted well over 2,000 trees. We have 30-some flowering plants in our prairies. And, as of last week, 165 different bird species have been identified at the Land Lab. So, we're creating massive amounts of diversity in this site and it just keeps improving.

…As the work got started, kids of all ages went out and planted trees. We had kindergarteners all the way up through high school and college students and even school board members out in the field planting trees together. We also reconstructed and excavated wetlands. At one time, this was a wetland area, so we broke field drainage tiles. And when you do that, wetlands show up. And when wetlands show up, the things that live in wetlands show up. We planted prairie plants in addition to planting trees. And when you plant prairies, you get prairies. And the things that use prairies—birds like short eared owls and northern harriers—show up. Especially in July and August, our prairies are absolutely stunning. As we planned the Land Lab, we did a lot of soil and hydrology work. We looked at topographic maps and found a historical stream that didn't exist anymore, so the students decided they wanted to restore it. With a lot of excavation work, we brought back Griffin's Run, which improved water quality downstream and created a new habitat for additional organisms to come take advantage of our Land Lab.

…Once you have something like this in place, amazing educational opportunities come along with it. One of the best parts is the constant influx of experts working side by side with my students. That gives them experiences well beyond anything I could do in the classroom on my own. Students have learned a lot about land and wildlife management. It's necessary to burn prairies, so we learned first-hand about fire as an ecological management tool. We've had lots of community support putting up structures like wood duck boxes and hawk posts. There are lots of birds, so we get birders from all over the place. Students also do research in the Land Lab. One of my favorite studies used a trail cam and captured an image of a mink feeding on a bullfrog. This is only the second time this situation has been recorded, so the students were able to publish a paper showing that mink feed on bullfrogs. It's always fun to see how students perceive the Land Lab. One way to get the student perspective is to have students keep field journals. Many different classes and subjects—things like art and writing—can be brought together in this way. Once the high school students are out there working with the experts, they can go on and share information with others, so we have college students mentoring high school students mentoring elementary students…all the way down to kindergarten. And that builds community support and gives the Land Lab a community feel.

…With the second half of the Land Lab, we did a few different things. We added an agroforestry section where we're growing crops for the cafeteria. We have maple syrup and honey. We have fruit trees that are going in, on top of the nut trees and more wild native trees already growing there. The students wanted to improve the accessibility of the Land Lab by building an observation deck overlooking one of the larger wetlands. They went out to look for funding and eventually got a local builder to meet them; they sketched out the plans over coffee. So now we have an observation deck that represents the collaboration of the entire community, not only the builders, but also groups like the Ohio Department of Natural Resources that chipped in to fund it. We've added signage—all of it designed by students—to make the area more accessible and educational for our community. I think the Land Lab represents a very bright tomorrow. I'm looking forward to the work that these students will do.

Anna Willow: All of this is absolutely amazing, and very different from a typical classroom. Thinking about the entire Land Lab project, what are you most proud of?

Jim Reding: Early on, I had a hard time getting students engaged in some of the ideas I was passionate about. They look at all the problems in the world and realize very quickly that they're not responsible for them. They're not the ones who created these problems in the first place. And they feel it's very difficult for them to make change. I learned that students had to be engaged in solutions; it wasn't enough to just talk about it. They had to do it. That's what the Land Lab represents. When I was bold enough to get out of their way and let them do what they wanted to do, it changed everything. As teachers, we're afraid to not have the answers, we're afraid to fail in front of students, and we're afraid to let students take control of our class. The Land Lab wouldn't have happened if I had given in to those fears. As a teacher, you have to just let them go. And they'll impress you when you do.

Anna Willow: Does that reflect your experiences and memories of the Land Lab, Dustin?

Dustin Braden: It absolutely does. As students in high school, we're told again and again, "You can make a difference. You can change the world." But at a certain point, we feel like, "Geez, I barely passed statistics. Can I really do any of this?" To have an opportunity to be told, "You can change the world...*now go do it*," that's an experience that I'd never had before I took Mr. Reding's class. So absolutely.

Anna Willow: I'd like to dream big for a moment. If you could have it your way, what would our educational systems and processes look like? What kind of things would students be learning? How would they be learning them? Certainly, some of this is reflected in the example of the Land Lab, but how we can replicate those beautiful experiences elsewhere? What might the next world of education look like?

Jim Reding: I have a 10-year-old son. And if you spend an hour with him, you'll understand that kids are incredibly curious. They never stop asking questions. They never stop having ideas. But by the time they get to high school, that flips. Sometimes it's like pulling teeth to get high school students to ask questions, talk, or collaborate. And it's not because they don't have ideas. It's because they've been trained to sit and get information and write it down. We take kids with a desire to learn and tell them what they need to know and then spend years convincing that that it is important. What we need to do instead is ask them what they want to know. What are they interested in? What do they want to do? I can't teach them everything, but I can help them find the answers. I can guide them by saying, "What do you need to know to do this?" and "Let's go figure it out together." When you put kids in charge of what they need to know, all of a sudden they're passionate about it. That's what I want to see for education. I want to be the facilitator. I want to be the one who says, "Here is some time, here are some tools, let's learn this together." So how do we do that? We have to teach the basic things, but math, history, English, and PE can all be covered in the first half of the school day. The rest of the day is theirs. Students can pick a project and do a deep dive into it. They'll find that they might need to know more about statistics or write a grant proposal in order to do what they want to do. But now there's a reason for it. There's passion behind it. If we give kids ownership over what they do, they will amaze us.

Anna Willow: Dustin, you're still a student yourself, about to graduate from college. In your view, what should our educational systems and processes look like? What have been the most meaningful aspects of your education?

Dustin Braden: We often forget that all learning is self-learning. If you don't have any reason or passion—if you've just been told that you need to memorize something, regurgitate it on a test, and be done with it—then why does any of it matter? In my year working at the Land Lab, I learned how to identify almost every tree species in Ohio. Hundreds of different bird species. Plant species. Suddenly things that never seemed relevant were *made* relevant by the project I was interested in. And I've never forgotten anything I learned working on those projects, because it had a meaning deeper than something I was just told I had to learn. So I agree that we need to think of teachers as facilitators and connect *why* there's value in learning something to *what* students are working on and passionate about.

Jim Reding: I have one thing to add to what Dustin said. Dustin is a great student and I'm sure he'll be graduating from his college with a great GPA. But what will make him a superstar going forward—and what will make him extremely marketable—are all of the other things he's done. Not the assignments in class, but the things he's done out of pure passion. The opportunities he has created for himself, where he found something he was interested in and dove into it. That's why he will be incredibly successful moving forward. We can teach content, but to be honest with you, you can find content on your phone. It's what you do with it that matters.

Anna Willow: What is stopping us from making these changes? What is keeping us from letting teachers be facilitators, letting students be leaders, and doing education in a project-based, experiential way? And what other challenges do we face when it comes to raising creative, connected kids?

Jim Reding: Although we argue that they are not as connected as they should be, I'm encouraged by the fact that this generation seems to see some value in nature. But, to me, one of the biggest problems is that students are driven to please their parents and please colleges. Parents want to see good grades. Colleges want to be able to say that everyone they admit scored well on standardized tests. And we are compared to other countries based on those tests. But standardized tests will not get us where we want to go. It's not the right measure. I had the opportunity to meet a bunch of teachers from Japan at a very eye-opening workshop. We met in Oregon and thought we were showing up to learn how *they* do it, so that we could do better here in the United States. And all they wanted to talk about is how *we* do it. They were kicking our butt on standardized tests, but saying that our students are better at creative thinking. Our students are better at problem solving and coming up with new ideas. We need to go with our strength. We need to get colleges to look at students not based on standardized tests but on what they actually *did* in high school. What is their body of work? What else do they bring to the table? What else can they do? Employers get it; they want to hire someone who can collaborate, communicate, problem solve, and think creatively. They will teach that person the content when they get there, but they need the initiative to use it. That matters so much more than grades. But that's not what will get you into college. That's a roadblock.

Dustin Braden: I totally agree. Right now, as I prepare to graduate, I'm applying for internships and jobs. And not a single position has asked what my GPA or standardized test scores were. Businesses don't want a robot who learned how to regurgitate facts. They want somebody who actually went out there, worked on projects, went above and beyond, and applied what they learned. We need colleges to do the same thing. Studies have shown that GPA and standardized test scores aren't reliable measures of success. We need to make sure colleges aren't just saying, "What's your GPA?" They need to ask, "What did you do?" and "How did you spend your time?" When students take on big projects, they get experiences and get to work with experts in their field of interest. And that's invaluable. Those experiences are really hard to get without changing how we measure things.

Anna Willow: As a young person interested in the environment and ready to devote your life to caring for it, where does that drive come from? Is it something that can be taught—whether in a classroom or a Land Lab—or does it come from somewhere else?

Dustin Braden: I think it absolutely can be taught and I can tell you who taught me: Mr. Reding and my father. But I definitely wasn't always like that. In middle school, I spent eight hours a day playing any videogame I could get my hands on. When I took Mr. Reding's class I can honestly say that I was interested in science, but I don't know that I was really interested in environmental issues, sustainability, and conservation. One thing we see is that a lot of people check out. Even people who are working in these areas get really pessimistic a lot of times. But finding ways to integrate solutions—like the Land Lab or school gardens—is how you teach people. It gets kids to realize that there are solutions to the problems their generation will have to face. There are solutions that they can get involved with right now. They don't have to wait until they graduate.

Jim Reding: There's an old adage that says the more you know about something, the more you care about it. And the more you care about something, the more likely you are to take care of it. It's always been my dream as a teacher to make environmental science mandatory for all graduating high school students in the state. We need to be educated. I think once you experience it in that intimate way, it's hard to walk away without wanting to do something. That's the hook.

Anna Willow: What do you see as our greatest areas of opportunity? Where can people who want to create a better world through education get started?

Jim Reding: Our young people are our greatest opportunity. They're willing, they're able, and they're capable. And, as adults, we have to welcome them. I used to be a pessimist. Now I'm an optimist. That's because of the students I get to work with every day. I think that is our best chance. We have a large population being educated, being informed, and becoming engaged. And they're moving ever closer to voting age. Unfortunately, things have gotten pretty scary out there in terms of environmental issues. Scary enough that it's forcing young people to say, "I've got to do something, and I've got to do it now." But the great thing is that they're willing to do it—youth who are willing to step up and adults who get out of their way or work with them.

Dustin Braden: In our area, we have great environmental education opportunities. It doesn't matter where you are; you can almost always find a park somewhere on your map. That's one great opportunity: The chance to get outside and connect—and get students out there as well. As far as what people can do, I think everybody is an expert on something. And as an expert, you can become a mentor. All of us have the opportunity to help somebody else up the ladder.

Anna Willow: It's obvious that you're an outstanding teacher, Jim. Do you think the average teacher can replicate your approach? Or is something like the Land Lab beyond what most teachers are capable of doing?[7]

Jim Reding: I would say it's not at all beyond what most teachers can do and I see myself as an average teacher. I think the difference is that at some point I decided I wasn't going to worry so much about the evaluation of myself as a teacher. My evaluation is not based on how well my kids score on a standardized test. It's based on how many environmental science professionals I create. On how many kids go out and do something that literally changes the world. I think that matters. I also think that as a teacher you've got to be willing to fail. Luckily, I've done enough of that in my life that I've gotten pretty comfortable with it. We've done some things that didn't work. And I was pretty confident that my job wouldn't be at risk because of it. That gives me some freedom, and I think it really changes the way I approach teaching. But given the opportunity, I think anybody can do it.

Anna Willow: Where does change come from in an educational setting? Does change come from parents? Does change come from students? Does it come from teachers? Does it come from administrators?

Jim Reding: That's a great question. I'd say it's a little bit of everything. There are certain expectations that come down from our district, and my principal has certain things he's looking for. Parents want what is best for their kids. They want students to be successful; they want them to enjoy the class, talk about it at the dinner table, and get a good grade. I do think a lot of changes come from students. Any teacher will tell you that some of the best conversations they've ever had in class were tangents, when a student asked a question and thirty minutes later everyone is still engaged in the answer. Some of the best days I've ever had were not on my lesson plans. We need to think back to when we were five, six, or seven years old and remember how to ask questions. We need to say, "Hey, we just talked about this, how does it relate to that?" That's the best education out there. That's the best learning.

---

[7] We would like to thank John Krieger for posing this and the subsequent question.

Students have the ability to drive that, but it will take everyone realizing that it's better than what we've been doing.

Anna Willow: Imagine being able to shift what we value in education, so we care about and measure success not as numbers on a test, but as the development of a person and their contributions to the world. That's what I would love to see in our next world. Any other ideas on how to make it happen?

Dustin Braden: I think a lot of kids are really scared of failure. People in my generation and younger are scared of looking stupid because we're told that we can't fail or that there will be negative consequences. Incorporating environmental content in a way that doesn't make students scared to fail will have students feeling more capable and more prepared to take on worldwide environmental issues. Because they built up that confidence. Their passion could be focused on environmental art or environmental writing—all necessary things for making environmental changes and addressing problems.

Jim Reding: For one thing, mentoring is incredibly valuable to kids. When a high school student works with kids in fourth or fifth grade, it validates their work. The other thing is that when we take students outside, we tend to plan and organize way too much. Just let them be outside! An elementary school teacher taking kids out for the day doesn't need four pages of lesson plans. They're going to learn. They're going to ask questions. Just get them outside! Let them enjoy it! Let them decide what they need to know. Let them identify the exciting things. One of the coolest things we do is give young kids cameras and say, "Go take pictures of something." That way, we see what they're excited about.

…One of the big things right now is project-based learning. In project-based learning, we let students start by asking themselves: "What do I want to do?" And then once they know what they want to do, the question becomes: "In order to do that, what do I need to know?" One of the things that has gotten really exciting for me is that a lot of students take my class because they heard that they will get to *do* something. They come to me and say, "This is what I wanna do for my project." They come in with an idea. That's what we need to shift, to ask the students "What do you want to do?" And, as teachers, we can help them along the path. My biggest role is getting out of their way. Giving them the tools and facilitating, but honestly getting out of their way and letting them do what they need to do. I think that changes things. I have seen it change things.

There needs to be a pretty serious overhaul in the education system. One of the main reasons we see divides in our country and internationally is that a lot of times we don't focus on change and new things. We focus on memorizing. But open-mindedness is going to be the key to transitioning into this next world and I believe this starts at the fundamental K-12 educational level.

~George, 11th Grade

We need more of an action focus. Going out and doing the things that you're talking about rather than just talking about them.

~Ella, 11th Grade

I think it's a lot easier to learn something when you've invested in it.

~John, 10th Grade

7
"The Moment We're In":
The Next World of Race Relations

The covid crisis, coupled with the exposure of police violence and the climate crisis, has created a time of reckoning in the United States. As journalist Anna North reminded us during the first wave of COVID-19 in mid-April of 2020,

> With every day that goes by, it becomes more clear that the virus isn't an equalizer at all. Instead, it is exacerbating the inequalities in American society, taking a disproportionate toll on low-income Americans, people of color, and others who were already marginalized before the crisis hit. While many white-collar workers can work from home, a disproportionate share of the front-line workers still going to their jobs in many industries are women and people of color. In Michigan, black residents made up around 40 percent of coronavirus deaths as of April 9, even though only about 14 percent of the population is black (North 2020).

While such statistics flashed like neon from the nightly news, it was the killing of George Floyd in Minneapolis, Minnesota—recorded on a teenager's cellphone—that forced America to look itself in the eye and pledge to change. With the memories of the deaths of Michael Brown, Treyvon Martin, Breonna Taylor, and so many others still hovering on the sideline of our national consciousness, George Floyd's murder stunned us anew. Despite some explosions of violence, it brought countless communities together for peaceful protests that spilled into the streets. Community members gathered together in each other's yards and church parking lots, where conversations held on simmer for decades began to boil again—often in productive ways. The question remains as to whether any true "next world" will emerge out of these ashes. Here and for now, we review the emotions and facts, struggles and insights, that will inform what happens next.

We can begin by recalling just how common deaths like George Floyd's have been in US history. A symbolic graveyard constructed in Minneapolis during the trial of Derek Chauvin, the police officer accused and eventually convicted of his death, served as a poignant reminder of the grim reality faced by many Black communities.[8]

As reported in *Yale News*, "over the past five years there has been no reduction in the racial disparity in fatal police shooting victims despite increased use of body cameras and closer media scrutiny" (Belli 2020). During the weeks of Chauvin's trial, *The New York Times* reported that at least 64 people in the US died at the hands of law enforcement, with Black and Latino people representing more than half of the dead (Eligon and Hubler 2021).

Since 2015, the *Washington Post* has kept a record of killings by police around the US, finding that such events take place much more frequently than they are reported in the news. In an investigation inspired by the 2014 shooting of Michael Brown, an unarmed Black

---

[8] This image is made publicly available through Creative Commons licensing on Wikimedia Commons. Wikimedia Commons contributors, George Floyd Square Minneapolis, MN Memorial to those killed by police (51402653868).jpg, *Wikimedia Commons,* https://commons.wikimedia.org/w/index.php?title=File:George_Floyd _Square_Minneapolis,_MN_Memorial_to_those_killed_by_police_(51402653868).j pg&oldid=589934498 (accessed February 3, 2022).

man, by police in Ferguson, Missouri, the *Post* found that "the FBI undercounted fatal police shootings by more than half. This is because reporting by police departments is voluntary and many departments fail to do so" (Tate et al. 2021). The rate at which non-white individuals (compared to their white counterparts) are killed is staggering. Out of a US white population of 197 million, 2,960 police killings were reported—a rate of 15 per million. This number rises for Hispanic Americans; out of a population of 39 million, 1,082 were killed in this manner—a rate of 28 per million. And for Black Americans, there were 1,550 police killings in a population of 42 million. This means that Black Americans were killed at a rate of 37 per million, which is more than twice the rate experienced by white Americans (Tate et al. 2021).

Adding to the injustice, very few officers are convicted by the grand juries weighing their cases. According to Philip Stinson, a professor in the criminal justice program at Bowling Green State University who studies civilian killings by members of law enforcement, "the most striking aspect of the statistics on lethal police force is how little the numbers have changed in the decade or two since researchers began to comprehensively track them. Even as cellphone videos and body cameras make it harder to hide human error and abuses of authority by law enforcement—and even as social media amplifies public outrage—only about 1.1 percent of officers who kill civilians are charged with murder or manslaughter" (Eligon and Hubler 2021). There are, of course, many layers to such statistics, as Stinson points out. Police are often in situations that require snap judgements under a lot of pressure, but the pattern remains consistent, and social justice advocates now call for a more expansive response, not only in police behavior but in public policy and the culture as a whole. As renown philosopher and social critic Cornel West told journalist Amy Goodman,

> We got social neglect. You've got economic abandonment. Every day, you've got poor black people who are wrestling with unbelievably oppressive conditions. And we've got to be able to speak candidly and honestly about that and come up with some ways of rechanneling a lot of this rage and anger (Goodman 2016).

Meanwhile, from the other end of the political spectrum, even conservative commentator David Brooks has weighed in, tracing the source of the disparate realities between races in this country:

> When we apply the lens [of empirical data] to African American experience we see that barriers to opportunity are still very high. The income gap separating white and Black families was basically as big in 2016 as it was in 1968. The wealth gap separating white and Black households grew even bigger between those years. Black adults are over 16 times more likely to live in families with three generations of poverty than white adults (Brooks 2021).

Brooks cites a 2004 study that likely still applies today, in which researchers sent equally qualified white and Black applicants to job interviews in New York City, dressed them similarly, and gave them similar things to say. Not surprisingly, Black applicants got half the number of callbacks or job offers as whites (Brooks 2021).

Such nods to the realities we face, from voices as disparate as West and Brooks, take us back to a place we thought we had passed long ago, when the Voting Rights Act, the War on Poverty and other such national agendas to correct long-standing injustices were so sorely needed. The changes we are now called to make run the gamut from the personal, the political, and the environmental to an end to the subtle microaggressions that continue to be part of the daily experience of many people of color. Stretch back to 1986, when journalist Brent Staples published a break-through essay entitled, "Just Walk on By: Black Men and Public Space" in *Harper's Magazine*, in which he reflects on his own experience of engrained bias:

> As a boy, I saw countless tough guys locked away; I have since buried several, too. They were babies, really—a teenage cousin, a brother of twenty-two, a childhood friend in his mid-twenties—all gone down in episodes of bravado played out in the streets. I came to doubt the virtues of intimidation early on. I chose, perhaps unconsciously, to remain a shadow—timid, but a

survivor. The fearsomeness mistakenly attributed to me in public places often has a perilous flavor. The most frightening of these confusions occurred in the late 1970s and early 1980s, when I worked as a journalist in Chicago. One day, rushing into the office of a magazine I was writing for with a deadline story in hand, I was mistaken for a burglar. The office manager called security and, with an ad hoc posse, pursued me through the labyrinthine halls, nearly to my editor's door. I had no way of proving who I was. I could only move briskly toward the company of someone who knew me.

...Relatively speaking, however, I never fared as badly as another black male journalist. He went to nearby Waukegan, Illinois, a couple of summers ago to work on a story about a murderer who was born there. Mistaking the reporter for the killer, police officers hauled him from his car at gunpoint and but for his press credentials would probably have tried to book him. Such episodes are not uncommon. Black men trade tales like this all the time. Over the years, I learned to smother the rage I felt at so often being taken for a criminal. Not to do so would surely have led to madness (Staples 1986).

When I've read these beautifully-written-but-terrifying passages with today's students, we are often collectively struck by their year of publication. From their perspective, 1986 seems so far away, but Staples' experiences echo and shatter across time to our present day. When we talk about changing the culture, we would do well to remember the experiences Staples recounts.

Everywhere we turn, we can trace such daily (though often hidden) disparities in our public lives. Consider the wide gap in school funding between rich and poor schools. Or the lack of quality food—or even a basic grocery store—experienced in many communities of color, as referenced by Shawn Jackson in the conversation below. Or the disproportionate percentage of income spent on energy by lower income households, a point discussed in Chapter 4 of this volume. Even something as "simple" as tree cover reveals severe splits from one community to the next. An environmental organization called American Forests features aerial photographs of different neighborhoods of the same city side by side on its website. The disparity between low and high-income areas is clear. Disadvantaged neighborhoods display the rooftops of densely packed homes and pavement is readily visible. Wealthier neighborhoods are filled with trees, which shade homes, regulate temperatures, and improve quality of life.[9]

As American Forests explains, "a map of tree cover in almost any American city is also a map of income. Simply put, lower-income neighborhoods usually don't have as many trees" (American Forests no date). Furthermore, lack of trees exacerbates social inequities, with fewer trees resulting in increased heat-related illnesses and lower air quality, which in turn lead to nearly 10,000 additional deaths each year in the US. Planting 31.4 million trees in cities each year would advance equity and slow climate change (American Forests no date).

Urban tree cover may seem a long way from the killings of Michael Brown, Breonna Taylor, and George Floyd, but layers of racial

---

[9]Aerial view of a Long Beach, California neighborhood, with few trees to be found. This image is made publicly available through Creative Commons licensing on Wikimedia Commons. Wikimedia Commons contributors, Hellman Neighborhood Long Beach California, *Wikimedia Commons,* https://commons.wikimedia.org/w/index.php?title=File:Hellman_Neighborhood_Long_Beach_California.JPG&oldid=465666220 (accessed February 3, 2022).

disparities run across all aspects of American life. All beg, together, for large-scale systemic change. Maybe such change begins by ensuring voting rights or lobbying legislatures to address the legacy of red-lining and housing discrimination. Or maybe it requires recognizing and undoing the implicit biases that trigger so many police shootings. From trees, to homes, to how we regard one another, all of these elements of our culture are being reengaged and renegotiated at this critical juncture in our history.

There is no clearer statement of the way racial disparities influence daily life than Claudia Rankine's 2014 book *Citizen*, in which she recounts her own stories along with those of other African Americans (celebrities and non-celebrities alike). Such disparities are on stark display in a story about a private encounter with a potential trauma therapist:

> The new therapist specializes in trauma therapy. We have only ever spoken on the phone. Her house has a side gate that leads to a back entrance she uses for patients. You walk down a path bordered on both sides with deer grass and rosemary to the gate, which turns out to be locked.
>
> At the front door the bell is a small round disk that you press firmly. When the door opens the woman standing there yells, as the top of her lungs, Get away from my house! What are you doing in my yard?
>
> It's as if a Doberman pinscher or a German shepherd had gained the power of speech. And you back up a few steps you manage to tell her that you have an appointment. You have an appointment? she spits back. Then she pauses. Everything pauses. Oh, she says, followed by, oh, yes, that's right. I am sorry.
>
> I am so sorry, so, so sorry (Rankine 2014:18)

The personal. The public. The communal. The traumatic. Where do we draw the line? On July 23 of 2020, we were joined by Reverend Marcia Dinkins, executive director of Ohio Interfaith Power and Light, and by

Pastor Shawn Jackson, who serves as both the pastor for Mayes Community Temple in Marion, Ohio and the Director of Student Life and Inclusion at Ohio State University's Marion Campus. As the conversation below reveals, structural racism forces us to question who we are as a people, how we listen (or don't listen) to each other, and how we can move from the troubling realities of today toward a more just and equitable next world. We cannot build a more inclusive economy, a more equitable distribution of wealth, and a healthier world for our families—nor can we address the increasingly destructive threat of climate change—unless we comprehend these dilemmas as conjoined. Injustice and all that goes with it must be met with a renewed sense of human solidarity and a deep and abiding empathy for "the moment we're in."

Anna Willow: Marcia and Shawn, we are so excited to have you here to talk about your work and your vision. Could you start us off with a bit of context about the work you've done to promote justice in central Ohio's communities?

Marcia Dinkins: For several years, I've been working on connecting issues at the state level to both the national and the local level. When I was leading a faith-based organization in Toledo, Ohio, I brought in a million dollars for a jobs program. I also worked to have an ordinance passed to reduce lead in our community, because children in Toledo had the second highest rate of lead poisoning. In addition to that, I've been working to give families a social safety net, which includes health care, food stamps, and food security. I've also done a lot of work around climate change and environmental justice, criminal justice reform, and been involved in ballot initiatives. I've done quite a bit over the years, and I think the best part is that I don't see my work as being fragmented, but as being one dimension with different layers inside of it.

Anna Willow: Shawn, could you tell us about the kind of work you've been doing to promote justice in central Ohio's communities? What have you been up to?

Shawn Jackson: Most of my work has been on the local level, in the Marion area. I stay pretty busy within my community. One of the organizations I'm involved in is the Marion Minority Commission, which was started in the early 2000s. I was one of the cofounders of the commission, which came together when a young child was killed in a drive-by shooting. The community was outraged, so we formed the commission to organize our community leaders, such as the police department, our mayor, and other city officials. One thing we do is help people of color know about relevant job openings within the community, especially so we can be represented in more influential positions downtown. I also work with the Black Heritage Council, which was created in about 1977 to raise scholarships for deserving minority students. Last year alone we gave out $8,000 in scholarships and we're in partnership with the Ohio State University. I'm proud that as a community we have these organizations.

Anna Willow: Thanks to both of you for sharing. This is wonderful work. The next question I want to ask is a rather large one. I'm going to ask you first, Shawn, to tell us what justice means to you. What does that word actually mean? What *is* justice? And if you could have it your way, if limitations were suddenly stripped away, what would our communities look like?

Shawn Jackson: That's a great question. I guess the first thing I think about is the grassroots. To have people willing to get in and put their hands to the plow through grassroots organizations. In our system, there are a lot of inequities when it comes to people who are considered Others. What we saw in 2008, with the election of our first Black president, was the beginning of folks showing their desire to see justice for all in this country. We need equal access and fairness across communities. Things such as jobs and education and healthcare and healthy food. Recently my church started an urban garden. This is in an area that is about four miles from the closest grocery store that sells fresh tomatoes and vegetables. That in itself is unequal. Justice, for me, is being able to participate in addressing those issues. Another thing that's really dear to my heart has to do with the penal system. We have over two million people in prison and over half of them are people of color, but Black people are about 13 percent of the country's population.

To address these kinds of issues is not to be out there fighting that fight by yourself. I got encouraged for the first time in a long time during the protests this summer [of 2020], to see that there were not only people from different races and ethnicities involved, but also generational differences as well. Young people were out there. There were high schoolers and middle schoolers out there who knew what they were doing. I got inspired by that. So that's what justice would look like to me. That when injustice is going on, we're willing to band together and say "an injustice for one is an injustice for all."[10]

Anna Willow: Marcia, what does justice mean for you? And if you could have it your way, what would just communities look like?

Marcia Dinkins: I think justice is one of those words that has several complex layers to it, because it is defined differently in different spaces. If you think about the church, there are people who seek justice in the church. There is justice that we seek in our community. There is justice that we seek nationally in the context Pastor Jackson just mentioned. When you think about the fight we're in, people are fighting not only for justice but also for visibility. And so, for me, justice is one of those words that you can look at subjectively or objectively and define in the moment. I don't know if I really want to take a stab at defining justice as much as I would like to define what's *inside* of justice, which is equality, equity, and need. Which then takes us to the movements that begin when people come to a place where they're reimagining what their communities could look like, what their lives could look like, and what a future could look like for their children and grandchildren. It's a place that gets you thinking about legacy, but it's also a place that begins to interweave your faith and your beliefs in a way that is no longer fracturing or traumatizing or retraumatizing, but is liberative. It's no longer oppressive. I don't want one life to be lifted above another. It's an exchange of respect. It's the fact that my life means just as much as the next life. Justice has to be defined accordingly.

---

[10] Here, Jackson is referencing Dr. Martin Luther King Jr.'s words. In his 1963 "Letter from a Birmingham Jail," King wrote that "injustice anywhere is a threat to justice everywhere. We are caught in an inescapable network of mutuality, tied in a single garment of destiny. Whatever affects one directly, affects all indirectly."

…And I don't want to marginalize the word. Justice goes much further and much deeper than what I could ever explain. To be honest, I take issue sometimes with the phrases *just economy* or *just world* because when we really think about it, the implications of that way of talking are more retributive than restorative. I'm not going to say we're all going to get along, but I'd like to live in a place where my grandchildren and my great-grandchildren can feel safe. I'd like to live in a place where my children can have the same books that the white schools have. I'd like for my children to learn about philosophy in their schools. I'd like a world where there is no Othering, where everyone deserves the same thing. I'd like to see patriarchy and supremacy—be it Black or white—buried. I'd like to see people join hand in hand and be interconnected and break the lines of our language and disrupt patterns that have continually perpetuated the trauma and division that the world is wrestling with now. Because if we had wrestled with this and reconciled with it a long time ago and asked these questions years ago, we wouldn't have books like *White Fragility*; we wouldn't have people trying to learn about white supremacy and working to develop a language so we can communicate with one another in order to bring about this revolution that people are building.

Anna Willow: One thing you said that particularly struck me is the importance of people reimagining what our communities could look like. So my next question for you is this: Where do you see evidence of this reimagined world? Where are pieces of it already in place that we can get excited about and inspired by?

Marcia Dinkins: I don't know that this world is here yet, but I do think it's being massaged. COVID-19 has been both a blessing and a burden to all of us. The blessing is that it has brought families back together. Community members are looking out for one another; neighbors are getting to know one another and people are putting cookies on your doorstep. People are caring about the needs of others. But it's also being massaged at a greater level: We see it in the protests, we see it in people grabbing books off the shelf to help them deal with white supremacy, to deal with the ancestral pain and stain, and seeking answers and ways to connect. And so, I think it's working its way through. People are realizing that the only way this blanket is going to be lifted is if we all grab a corner and lift it. And they are now trying to do just that. People are looking at privilege and saying, "I realize how white people get privileged." Those are some of the things I see happening. And it does invoke our imagination. It does promote our curiosity, because now I want to get deeper into you, into them, into us, into we.

Anna Willow: Shawn, where do you see evidence of the next world? Where are things working well?

Shawn Jackson: What Marcia said really resonated with me. It's being able to have a radical imagination. When I say radical imagination, I'm talking about having the courage and the intelligence to recognize that the world can and should be changed. Up to this time, people haven't really recognized that we're living in a world that's broken. We're living in a society that doesn't treat everyone as though they're valued. The radical imagination that I'm talking about is not just about dreaming of different futures; it's about acknowledging that those futures can be ours. And it is about bringing those possibilities back from the future to work on the present to inspire action and new forms of solidarity today. I'll come back once again to when I was watching, participating, and standing back during some of the protests that happened here in Marion, Ohio [in the summer of 2020]. The younger generation did not need me, a 55-year-old man who everybody normally expects to be out there leading the charge. A new generation is coming with better ideas, more complete ideas, that we're getting ready to live out. That's what I'm excited to see. I see evidence of the next world in our capacity to imagine and make a common cause with the experiences of other people. It undergirds our ability to build solidarity across boundaries and borders. That's the basis of solidarity: If we're ever going to come together as a people and value people no matter where they come from or who they love, we need to show people respectful love regardless of those things.

…One of the things that got me involved with our urban garden was when a councilman presented land to us from a land bank. As a pastor in a community that is predominantly Appalachian white, I saw an opportunity. Our church is about 98 percent African American. It has been there since 1992, and I probably knew around two of the community members. There are a lot of cultural differences, so it was very difficult to find something to connect with people when we would go to their doors and say, "Hey, would you like to come to our church sometime?" But when we got this land bank opportunity I started thinking that this might be a chance to connect with our community, because you can always do that around food. We're talking about using our imagination, our courage, and about evidence of the next world. Evidence of that new world would be a few white folks coming to a predominantly Black church in a predominantly Appalachian white community and planting food to make a garden successful. Part of it would be a transformation of what once was a blighted area—an empty lot where a house was torn down—into a flourishing green space.

Anna Willow: I want to turn to Marcia and ask a question about challenges. What do you see as the biggest challenges we need to overcome in order to make these positive visions a reality?

Marcia Dinkins: There needs to be a change in culture. Let's take, for example, George Floyd's situation. Let's take the protesters. What are they fighting against? What are they calling for? Defund the police. I've said to people over and over again that it's not always training that police need—you have to break up the culture. Because culture sits silently in rooms. It does not announce itself. It does not show up. People do not always recognize it, so we point the finger at different things that could be tweaked and made better. But at the end of the day, it's culture. It's the culture that continues to block us. It's the culture that continues to stifle us. It's the culture that continues to run rampant in our communities. And because of that, it's also used against us. Think about overpolicing of Black and Brown bodies. Think about [immigrant] children who are in detention camps and parents who are being separated from their children. It comes down to the culture of the people who are making the laws. And the fear. Until we can get over those two things, we're always going to have this subset of challenges. What they're using against us is culture. They're pitting us against one another. How? Culture. Until we can change the culture of policing; how they feel education should be; the way they view Black and Brown bodies, Black and Brown women and children, and other people who are not part of the elitist system; and the culture of elitism, we're going to continue to face these challenges. We need to recognize it at all levels, not just on one level, but on *every* level. It's a start. It's not our destination.

Anna Willow: As an environmental anthropologist, I've spent most of my career studying culture. But in recent years I've gone from studying culture to trying to change it, so I completely understand and agree with what you said. On the flip side, Marcia, what do you see as our biggest opportunities? What can people like us do to put these positive next worlds into place?

Marcia Dinkins: I think we have to confront ourselves. We have to confront our truths and our biases. We have to confront our own culture; our own way of thinking and being, and begin to move from a system of *self* to a system of *us*. Until we can confront who we are, things will continue to be the same. I think it starts there. We have to be transparent in that. And then we have to get out of the way. You know, a lot of times our own thoughts, premises, and perceptions get in the way and hinder where we're trying to go. I believe change will come once we can confront ourselves and tell our own stories reasonably, truthfully, and transparently—and allow our stories to connect to other people. At the same time, we need to let other people have their own stories and tell them the way they want. It's about meeting and respecting people where they are. Until we learn how to love honestly, wholeheartedly, truthfully, transparently, and without judgement, we're not going to get anywhere anyway. So I think the first thing we can do is love ourselves, love one another, and let that love turn radical. And build from that. That's when we will begin to see real justice, because love is going to dig deep. Love isn't going to judge. And believe it or not, we talk about institutional and structural systems and all of that, but we have to look at these other systems. Systems of belief, systems of language. We need to learn how to talk to one another. And hear one another. Those are things that we can do. And then we can build together.

Anna Willow: Shawn, what is your answer to that question? What can people like us do?

Shawn Jackson: One thing we need to do is talk to our children and grandchildren about racial inequities and social injustice. I think sometimes we act as though those things are not prevalent in our society.

I'm speaking to you as an African American male who has been in many conversations—at the barber shop or at work—with white people who make comments like, "We've come a long ways" or "I thought that was all behind us." Comments like that show that there is no real awareness, and many times Black and Brown people are not having those conversations with white people. So it's very important when you have a relationship with someone who's different from you to take advantage of it. Don't be afraid to ask to have those conversations. Learn how to be comfortable being uncomfortable. We need to reeducate ourselves. In particular, I would encourage white folks to educate themselves about the hard history of the United States, which was developed through slavery and inequity from minute one. It's important that we address those issues. And we need to look for opportunities right now to have those conversations with our friends, on the job, and with our family members. We need to have those conversations, make sure people feel comfortable having them, and find out where people are at.

Anna Willow: So often people are afraid of saying or doing the wrong thing. How do we help people feel comfortable and get them having these essential conversations?

Shawn Jackson: We first have to get permission. Once you have a relationship, people you are friends with will be able to tell if you are truly curious or if you mean ill. Ask them if it's okay. Say, "I need to ask you a question. I feel very uncomfortable and I don't want to hurt you by asking this." You'll know how to craft it.

Marcia Dinkins: To add to that, we have to realize that America is in a moment that it's never been in before. And that means that white people who have roots embedded in racism and white supremacy have never had to have these conversations before. They never had to have these conversations in their homes or their churches, or anywhere else, so they never learned the language to communicate about these things. What's happening now is that people are trying to figure out how to have these conversations. This is why there's fear—because we've never had to do this before. Many white people are asking, "How do I show up in a space that I've really never had to pay attention to? How do I show up in a space that I never had to look at and see that it was something divisive or harmful because my world was different?" We have to remember that in many households all of this was just normalized behavior without ever giving it the term racism. It was just a way of living. It was about being a good Republican or a good evangelical or coming from a good family and living in a good community. These things were givens that just went down the generational line. So now people have to pay attention to something they never had to pay attention to before. That's why it's so difficult. And because it's such a heated moment, it is also creating fear and angst. People don't know how to confront it because they don't know what's going to happen. So many people are wondering, "How do I show up? How do I show my sincerity without being pushed back, bullied into a corner, or told there's nothing you can do?" And we have to make space for that. And we have to give grace for that.

Anna Willow: I've often heard white people claim that they don't see things in racial terms or that being "colorblind" is the best solution. But I've heard from Black colleagues that this is problematic. What do you think? What's wrong with saying "I don't see color?"

Marcia Dinkins: We *do* see color. I think it should be more like, "I see color, but I don't judge by it." There's a difference. When you look at me you see a Black woman, let's keep it real. When I look at you, I see a white woman. What I *don't* do is treat you differently based on what I see. That's what we have to realize. We do see color. It's just like somebody saying, I don't see men and women. You do. We've been socialized to see these things. So you can see me as a Black woman, but not treat me in a way that is racist, judgmental, or disrespectful. See me for who I am, but also respect me for who I am. And realize that there should be no separation between us. That's what we have to realize. It's okay to see color.

Shawn Jackson: The reality is that, as a Black man, my experiences are going to be totally different than a white man's. Those stereotypes and images are there. We need to be transparent, as Marcia said. We just need to be honest.

Anna Willow: One last question: Right now it feels like important changes are happening. How hopeful are you that real change will take place during this time of crisis and unrest?

Marcia Dinkins: We've talked about being honest, so I'm going to be honest. I'm hopeful, but I'm also fearful. Because we're still at a point of unrest. We're still at a point where people are being pulled over in cars and being beat up and brutalized. I am scared because sometimes we can push for so much that we compromise…and then what we've compromised comes back to bite us or hurt us later. I am hopeful because I believe that if we really do band together we can make change. Substantial change takes time. The struggle is real. We have to remember that we didn't get to this place yesterday. We didn't get to this place when George Floyd died. It was created through a set of laws and policies long before and beyond all of this. So again, I'm hopeful, but I am also fearful. My hope is that instead of treating others like we've been treated, we find a way to come together and be healed. Slowly and sustainably.

I think one of the most important things is equal opportunities for people of different social backgrounds, to give everyone the chance to make something of themselves. The opportunities now are very specific, and if we could make it so that everyone had access to a good education and the college system that would be a good place to start.
~Ella, 11th Grade

8
Democracy Unchained

As Nathaniel Rich recently explained, we had the chance to solve the climate crisis 30 years ago, when NASA administrator James Hansen warned Congress about the dangers global warming would unleash. Nearly immediately, democratic forces in the US government came together to tackle the emerging crisis, with consensus on both sides of the aisle. In the fall of 1988 alone, "32 climate bills [were] introduced in Congress," along with "an omnibus National Energy Policy Act, cosponsored by 13 Democrats and five Republicans" (Rich 2018:51). Even executives at Exxon appeared ready to chime in, says Rich; it was a moment when "the environmental movement, in the words of one energy lobbyist, "was on a tear"" (2019:51).

It is now clear, however, that other forces coalesced around a very different agenda: Salvaging as much time for fossil fuel industries to eke out every drop of money they could from their endeavors, lest the world they had built for us—composed of superhighways, acres of parking lots, the denigration of train travel, long commutes to work, mounds of plastic packaging, and cornfields lathered with petroleum-based fertilizers—cease to continue. Never mind that those same fossil fuels were stoking global warming that would threaten that very civilization. Like Midas holding onto his special powers, the fossil fuel industry would seek ever more destructive ways to pull oil out of the ground, including tar sands mines that have clear-cut areas in western Canada the size of England (Nikiforuk 2010), methane-producing fracking operations (Wilber 2012; Gold 2014), and deep ocean drilling of the kind that contaminated the Gulf of Mexico with oil spilling from submerged wells operators were unable to cap for months (Klein 2014). Looking back, it shakes one's soul to realize we might have done better, but for the political will to follow another path.

Now we sit on the edge of a different precipice, trying to imagine how we might mend a democracy so polarized that it has become dysfunctional. In many ways, the split runs between those who want to continue with the support of fossil fuel companies, which are subsidized worldwide at the staggering rate of $10 million a minute (Hawken 2017:3), and those who would seek other, more regenerative means of structuring culture (e.g., Klein 2014; Wahl 2016; Hopkins 2019). Many, including the experts featured in this volume, are wondering if democracy, linked as it so often is to capitalist structures, is up to the task (see Chapter 9).

On September 16, 2020, we were joined by Joel Wainwright and David Orr, both leading contemporary thinkers on the intersection of climate change and democracy. In his recent book, *Climate Leviathan* (co-authored with Geoff Mann), Wainwright asks whether the same political structures that produced our fossil-fueled emergency can be expected to solve it (Wainwright and Mann 2018). With so many competing forces, do we have enough time to work it all out, as democratic debates and conversations require? Wouldn't it be better, Wainwright and Mann wonder out loud, if some "big world force" (i.e., a Climate Leviathan) came in and told us how to fix the problem, directing multinational companies to behave with foresight and governmental decisions to toe the line toward the changes needed? While Wainwright and Mann fear such draconian action, they ponder its necessity. If not a Climate Leviathan, then perhaps an authoritarian, anti-capitalist power—what they term Climate Mao—could apply an even firmer hand. Modern China, capable of connecting a wide range of cities with trains and "stopping General Motors' gas-guzzling Hummer" in one fell swoop (Wainwright and Mann 2018:40-84), offers an example. Neither of these possibilities sound all that appealing. But how else can we avoid the chaos of a third option—one Wainwright and Mann call the Climate Behemoth—where the irresponsibility of climate-denying industries and governmental factions and their loyal followers send us running toward the brink of the worst effects of this crisis (Wainwright and Mann 2018:168)?

Others, such as David Orr, make the converse claim that only by creating a stronger democracy can we move toward robust national climate policy. In his introduction to *Democracy Unchained: How to Rebuild Government for the People*, Orr argues that "achieving [a] more inclusive and wiser country will…require advances in the art and science of democratic governance," and asks, "instead of self-defeating gridlock between warring factions, can we learn to act in concert to protect our common wealth of air, water, lands, biological diversity, and the values of truth, justice, and decency that we hold in common?" (2020:11). Aware that democracy has never operated in an equitable fashion nor truly represented the needs and voices of all people, Orr proposes that a vast majority of Americans want greater equity, higher taxes for the ultra-wealthy, and would prefer not to be "breathing filthy air, drinking polluted water, eating chemically saturated food or living in a much hotter and more capricious climate" (2020:8). Unfortunately, our current structure makes these basic wishes pale in the face of pressures applied by "K street lobbyists" (Orr 2020:8). What if we plunged in and applied the kind of "weaver politics" that conservative columnist David Brooks recommends in his essay "The Future of American Politics?" Brooks imagines a "politics of weaving [that would grow] out of the acknowledgment that there is no dominant majority in America. There is no moderate center. Your group will never pulverize and eliminate your opposing group. There's no choice but to set up better collaborative systems across difference. This is not a problem, it's an adventure" (Brooks 2020).

To embrace this adventure, as both Orr and Brooks would likely agree, will require a major national endeavor, tackling the ingrained practices that have long-thwarted true one-person-one-vote rule or have been put in place by people fearful of allowing such rule. Journalist Andrew Gumbel catalogues various elements of the modern-day assault on voting:

- Overzealous purging of the voter rolls
- Capricious restrictions on registration requirements
- Elimination of early voting days
- Intolerable delays and omissions in sending out absentee ballots
- Excessively long lines at polling stations
- Aggressive gerrymandering of state and congressional districts
- And perhaps most insidious, the insistence in many states that

voters present valid government ID, a policy that seemed incontrovertible on its face but in practice penalizes the poor, the elderly, and the transient—many of them racial minorities (Gumbel 2020:59-60).

Consider the following two examples of the now-standard practice of gerrymandering deployed to keep ruling parties in power, one from Republicans in Ohio and the other from Democrats in Maryland:[11]

Such blatant manipulation is obvious to all as a misuse of true democratic principles, as are the oil and gas industry's financial contributions to climate-denying legislators in Washington and around the country. Such contributions have increased substantially over the past thirty years, with contributions to Republican legislators dominating the field. In 1990, Republican legislators received under ten million dollars from the oil and gas industry. This ballooned in the 2010s, reaching over 50 million dollars in the 2012 and 2016 election cycles. It is worth mentioning that Democratic legislators also received oil and gas contributions, which held steady under ten million dollars over the thirty-year period (Kusnetz 2020).

---

[11] These images are made publicly available through Creative Commons licensing on Wikimedia Commons. Ohio: Wikimedia Commons contributors, Ohio Congressional Districts with party colors, 2013-2015, *Wikimedia Commons,* https://commons. wikimedia.org/w/index.php?title=File:Ohio_Congressional_Districts_with_party_col ors,_2013-2015,_unlabeled.svg&oldid=507491103 (accessed February 3, 2022). Maryland: Wikimedia Commons contributors, 2020 U.S. House elections in Maryland, *Wikimedia Commons, the free media repository,* https://commons. wikimedia.org/w/index.php?title=File:2020_U.S._House_elections_in_Maryland.svg &oldid=591304226 (accessed February 3, 2022).

With legislators continually desperate for financial contributions to keep themselves in office, it is difficult to imagine our democratic institutions working against their own interests by passing laws that would threaten the very funders who keep them in power. As Naomi Klein and others have made clear, the richest people on the planet have all the money they need to keep such contributions alive and growing (2014:44-45). Attempts to reason with such vested interests appear futile. Jane Mayer, in her ground-breaking book, *Dark Money: The Hidden History of the Billionaires Behind the Rise of the Radical Right*, reviews such attempts, referencing Michael Mann, a climate scientist who helped orchestrate Barack Obama's climate policies:

> By choosing a moderate, bipartisan approach, the Obama administration and many environmentalists assumed a deal would be winnable. "What we didn't take into account," Mann later noted, "was the ferociousness of the moneyed interests and the politicians doing their bidding. We are talking about a direct challenge to the most powerful industry that has ever existed on the face of the earth. There's no depth to which they're unwilling to sink to challenge anything threatening their interests" (Mayer 2017:199-200).

Clearly, the forces set against a working democracy that can address climate change and other large-scale challenges are very strong. Yet some scholars offer hope. Even Wainwright and Mann, skeptical as they are of solving such crises in time, call for "a transformation of the political," asking "by what paths we might undertake political transformations required for something like a just and livable planet?" (Wainwright and Mann 2018:28). Beyond Climate Leviathan, Climate Mao, and the horrors of Climate Behemoth, they conjure a "Climate X," where "the great majority of the world's population (not just the elites and the ecologically conscious middle-class individuals) understand the implications, relate these implications to their own lives, and actively…participate in the global effort of stabilization'" (2018:178, drawing on Li 2009).

Can we imagine a situation in which more and more people realize where we are and are willing to work toward change? Some would say we are already there, and that the majority of Americans support strong climate measures. As legal scholar Tim Wu affirms, "the defining political fact of our time is not polarization. It's the inability of even large bi-partisan majorities to get what they want" (quoted in Orr 2020:8). Andrew Gumbel also supports such an analysis:

> The good news…is that while voters may *start* from the position that the other side is irredeemably corrupt and hell-bent on cheating, they also generally support the notion that control of the electoral process should be taken out of the parties' hands and made fair and uniform for all. They like early voting and other conveniences, regardless of party. In a number of ballot initiatives around the country, in red states as well as blue, they have voted to curtail the power of big money and end gerrymandering, and they have voted, too, in favor of ranked-choice voting, which tends to favor moderate, consensus-seeking candidates over hyper-partisan ones. And, yes, they'd be happy to make Election Day a federal holiday (Gumbel 2020:71).

If Li, Wu, and Gumbel are right, maybe the real responsibility for bringing democracy to life—in ways never before realized, serving all ranges of people and positions, parties, and possibilities for solving the issues before us—lies not with those in power, who have so much to lose, but with all of us—the people in this country and around the world—who have "a planet to win" (Arnoff et al. 2019). As David Orr and Joel Wainwright show in the following conversation, the stakes could not be higher.

☼

Anna Willow: Both of you have authored important books that tackle the intersections of climate change and political systems. Can you provide us with a quick summary of your main message and why this topic matters so much right now? David, let's start with you.

David Orr: Let me say three things. First, it would be hard to identify any major problem that we face—climate change, equity issues, urban renewal—that doesn't trace back to some failure of democratic institutions. It would be hard to name a problem—a major problem—that our democracy has solved in the past 50 years. Second, the title *Democracy Unchained* is taken from the inversion of Nancy MacLean's book *Democracy in Chains*. Unchained from what? Unchained from the racism, militarism, and oligarchy foreseen long ago in *The Federalist Papers*. Third, we have never really been democratic. Many decisions are made outside the public purview. The role of money is incredible. In our society, the bridge that ought to connect our public opinions and feelings with public policy, regulations, and laws has been rendered a toll bridge accessible only to the wealthy. I believe that solving issues such as climate change will require us to build a true democracy.

Anna Willow: Later on I'll ask you how we can do that. Joel, please tell us about the main message of your work and the points you wanted to get across in *Climate Leviathan*.

Joel Wainwright: *Climate Leviathan* was co-authored with my friend and colleague Geoff Mann, who teaches at Simon Fraser University in Canada. Geoff and I were motivated to try and answer a question that kept coming up in conversations we were having around the time of the Copenhagen meeting [COP15], which took place in December 2009, one year after the election of Barack Obama. At that time, a lot of people in the so-called progressive environmental movement really believed that Obama would sweep in and create a new global climate change agreement that would get things under control. Obviously, that didn't happen. We wanted to understand more fully not only why it failed, but also the limits of thinking in the environmental movement about how to change the global political system. And alongside that, we asked another question, which wasn't all that acceptable ten years ago, but which seems like a commonsense question today: In the event that so-called democratic (or, more properly, capitalist democratic) societies fail to quickly decarbonize and thereby fail to address the climate crisis, what was going to happen politically? What is a reasonable expectation about where things would go? On the one hand, our book is a Marxist political analysis of the difficulty capitalist states have addressing the politics of climate change. On the other hand, we ask where the world is going. Thus, it's a book about the future and the future possibilities of the organization of political life.

...There's no way I can do justice in this brief time to the *Climate Leviathan*'s argument, except to say that what Geoff and I claim is most likely to emerge is a pathway that would allow for many different types of political arrangements that we call "climate Leviathan," in homage to Thomas Hobbes—usually not someone Marxists write about. To make a long story short, we think the world is going to remain capitalist, which means it's not going to be able to deal with decarbonization, but that we're going to go through what we call an *adaptation* of the political. A rearrangement of political life which will move even further away from what we might think of as true democracy and towards something we call planetary sovereignty. In other words, our prognoses are very dire. And we make no bones about this. Nevertheless, what we're calling for is a kind of revolutionary alternative, which begins with some very simple principles. Namely, that we need to go back to the basic question of what democracy could look like and rebuild from the ground up.

Anna Willow: Many people see democracy as a complex concept. And, as you were just saying, it may not be exactly what we should be striving for, at least not as we've come to understand it. So, Joel, what does democracy mean to you? If you could have it your way, what would our political system look like?

Joel Wainwright: Great question. If I could quibble with the premise behind it, though, I don't think the concept of democracy is that complicated. As far as I can tell, people everywhere have more or less the same understanding of what it means. The reason for the confusion is that we mix up formal and substantive conceptions of democracy. The latter is essential, the former is epiphenomenal. A formal conception of democracy defines it in terms of procedures. For instance, we're taught in the United States that because we have free and fair elections where, in theory, everybody gets one vote, we're a democratic society. Whereas other societies that lack those minimal requirements are not democracies. This is obviously really dumb, because merely having elections with votes doesn't guarantee anything like liberty for all or equality.

…The simple definition of democracy I prefer comes back to the substance of it. Any relationship is democratic to the extent that all of the members of the group or community could in theory lead. That's it. For instance, let's say you're in a two-person relationship and you genuinely respect the other party. In theory, on just about any important matter, you could trust the other person to take the lead. Or consider a student organization, or a group of friends trying to make a decision about whether to have pizza, go out for Chinese food, or stay home. If one person always gets to make the decision, it is not a democratic relationship. If you could pick at random who decides, it is democratic. The same could be true of political societies. I put it to you that our society is a long way from meeting this ideal, because there are many mechanisms in place—beginning with the massive inequalities in wealth, power, and opportunity—that prevent anything close to a genuinely democratic political society.

Now to answer the last part of your question about how our political systems could look: I actually think all of us have experienced democracy in our lives. It's just that we do so on relatively small scale, when relationships are based on respect for the other and mutual recognition of the need to share resources. I hope and believe that all of you have loving relationships in your life that are basically democratic. It's simply that we don't have enough of them, particularly on a large scale.

Anna Willow: David, we've heard Joel's response. I'm curious to learn what democracy means for you. And if you could have it your way, what would the political systems of tomorrow look like?

David Orr: I think democracy entails a change in language. In a purely economic or consumerist view of the world, the operative pronouns are "I," "me," and "mine." Democracy requires a public language and a shift to "we," "ours," and "us." It is about "we, the people." That requires a decision about who "the people" are and drawing boundaries around the constituent group that votes and participates. This change of language establishes how we think about our relationships in society.

The biggest problem with democracy in the United States is, as Joel pointed out, the uneasy relationship between the reality of capitalism, how we are governed, and how public business is actually done. We often assume that democracy and capitalism are in some way synonymous, or necessary to each other, or flip sides of the same coin. I don't think so. I think this is a very uneasy cohabitation, for many of the reasons noted by Adam Smith in *The Wealth of Nations* (2010 [1776]). Capitalism on its own tends toward crisis, monopoly, and conspiracies between capitalists and the larger society. In our own history, the 14th Amendment passed after the Civil War was aimed to liberate persons of previous servitude. In fact, it was hijacked by corporate lawyers, so the law played itself out through successive supreme court decisions, from 1886 to the present, by which the Court gave the rights of persons to corporations. You and I are persons. We're mortal. We can only be in one place at a time. We have limited assets. Eventually we die. We have moral commitments. Corporations have none of those. The characteristics of corporations are rather like those of a sociopath. To say that a corporation has the same rights that you and I do is simply a mistake, yet we operate a government built very much around the rights of corporations.

…What would a true democracy look like? That's a great question. Let me start with just two points. First, for all its imperfections, democracy is the only system of governance that we know of that routinely aims to protect the dignity and rights of its citizens. In a democracy, we have rights, "unalienable" rights in the words of the Declaration of Independence. Those rights say you and I matter, that we have dignity. So that's where democracy would begin and that's what sustains it. And that's why it's worth defending. In authoritarian societies, where dissidents and persecuted minorities can be hauled off to a prison, the individual has no rights and the law doesn't matter.

…Second, we're in the middle of a climate crisis. It is not something that will happen someday. The effects are building year by year. Forests in the West are burning tonight and dual hurricanes are hitting the Gulf Coast. Sea levels have been rising, oceans are acidifying, species are going extinct. And yet, you could destroy the planet, as oil companies and fossil fuel owners are doing, and never break a law. Let me repeat that: There are no existing laws being broken as Exxon, Mobil, and BP execute their plans to sell their inventory of fossil energy. Doing so will destroy your future—and not break a law. There's nothing democratic about that. And so, this large policy decision hangs over us. The democracy that we have to envision must be powered by efficiency and sunshine. Combustion of coal, oil, and gas must be made a crime because it is. We have to disinvent fire, as Amory Lovins once said (see Lovins 2011). To get there, we have to make that toll bridge a bridge of democracy, where everybody has a say—and that includes generations to come. That means that money generated from selling fossil fuels could no longer corrupt our politics. *Citizens United*, the Supreme Court decision, must be undone. All elections for federal or even state offices ought to be paid for publicly.

Anna Willow: You've told us and you've written that strengthening democracy is essential if we're going to truly start addressing climate change. Is it really as simple as that? Can we simply vote for people who will change the laws so that shareholder profits and greed are no longer paramount? Or do you have something else in mind?

David Orr: There are a lot of things. If we were to list what has to happen to have a functioning democracy, that list would include equity. Joel's point about inequitable distribution of wealth is fundamental here. The founders of this country lived in a middle-class/poor agrarian society. We live in a society that is basically an oligarchy. There are four or five people in the United States with more wealth than the bottom 90 percent. You cannot have a democracy with extremes like that. Furthermore, the Constitution and Bill of Rights say nothing about voting. You and I have no constitutional right to vote. It is simply assigned to states, and the states have implemented very different ways to manage voting. The right to register an opinion about who governs, by what terms, and to what ends is the core assumption of democracy. I live in a congressional district that is gerrymandered to ensure the election of one of the most extreme right-wing members of Congress. Republicans have gotten very good at it and very deliberate about it, but Democrats also draw partisan electoral districts. The right to vote has got to be guaranteed. Prior to Georgia's 2018 gubernatorial election, the Secretary of State eliminated tens of thousands of people from the eligible rolls in order to win by a very narrow election. The right to vote has got to be guaranteed. We need to systematize the whole voting process, so that voting becomes a holiday and easy to do.

Anna Willow: We are here to talk about what we hope our next world will be like and how we can bring that world into reality. Where do you see evidence of things working well?

David Orr: That's a tough question. There are lots of little places where things work well, but they're not working well at scale in this country right now. If I live in Montana, my vote counts for a whole lot more than somebody living in California. Montana has three people and 30 million cows. California has nearly 50 million people and six cows. They both elect two senators, so if you live in Montana, your vote in the senate counts for a great deal. The way we chose presidents through the electoral college subverts democracy and privileges rural people. The system no longer accords with a country of 331 million mostly urban people. Democracy does work well in certain pockets, where people are highly responsive to public issues and participate actively. In my opinion, that's why climate change has become a global crisis. We waited until the last minute to act. It is not likely to be solved by the people who control the US government. It won't be solved by corporations. It will require a fully functioning and effective democracy.

…That is the challenge before our generation, your generation. We've got to make a democratic society work and make it effective, transparent, and accountable. We know what must be done. We must be prepared to cause what the late John Lewis called "good trouble." Necessary trouble, with great decency, fairness, and justice. You'll encounter resistance. John Lewis' skull was fractured by police at the Pettus Bridge. And his life was spent fighting death threats and all kinds of things, but he persevered. The good work ahead of us is to create that democracy. Fairness, decency, and justice. That's the challenge. And now we have to do it at something close to a global scale. The good news is that the public is with us. A very high percentage of people want fairness, want to participate. I think a lot of the hard-core right-wing opposition is quite understandable: It's people who feel left out of the system. That's why it's so necessary to bring *everybody* along.

Anna Willow: Joel, it's your turn to tell us where in the world you see things working well.

Joel Wainwright: David gave us an extremely elegant and clear description of American democracy's problems. It wasn't the full catalogue; as far as the US is concerned, we could go on about these problems all night. But let's take a broader look. Let's look at the world as a whole. The world in, say, 2005, was by no means perfectly democratic. I think we all know that. But what is striking is that since around 2008-2009, the world has taken a hard shift to the right. Not many people predicted this, and there's really no clear theory or widely accepted understanding of why this has happened. To give you a sense of what I'm talking about, let's run through a few examples. You have the rise of men like Berlusconi in Italy, Modi in India, Abe in Japan, Putin in Russia, Bolsonaro in Brazil, and of course Trump here in the United States. It's happened in one large country after another, in every one of those cases—and there are others. We could also include Brexit in the UK. In most of those cases, if you roll the tape back and listen to what people were saying two or three years before those figures took power, mainstream opinion views them as clownish, buffoonish, with no chance of victory. They are seen as adopting a politics that is so extreme right, so loaded with racism and sexism and homophobia that they can't possibly be taken seriously. And in every case, that person wins and then puts in place an extremely authoritarian state that, among other things, attacks the mechanisms usually associated with democratic society. Let me be candid: Not only do we have a poor understanding of why this is happening, we also lack mechanisms to roll it back. The phenomenon represented by Donald Trump is not going away. There is a hard-core one-third of our society that believes and will continue to believe that their politics are virtuous and that they need to continue to attack. And it may be that in four years we're confronted by a new figure who represents the same kind of extreme right politics but who is in fact more suave, more capable of presenting the politics in a way that is compelling to middle Americans. We've seen this in other parts of the world.

…Now, to look for utopian spaces where people are avoiding all of this is challenging for the very simple reason that I just talked about, the emergence of what some call "authoritarian populist" leaders of powerful capitalist states. The states at the top of the world's power hierarchy are some of the largest, most powerful, biggest economies; they set the rules, they set the norms. No place is immune. Even if I could tell you, for instance, "there are amazing villages in Kerala' (India) or "I've spend time in the Zapatista region of Chiapas (Mexico) and it's just incredible," where would that take us? We live in a global political system.

I take hope from the fact that there are places where well-rooted democratic social movements are confronting authoritarian forms of power and trying, as David suggested, not only to reinforce the existing neoliberal parties, but also to reach to the masses—who so often invest their hopes and desires and dreams in fascistic or extreme right leaders—and show them a radical politics that would take them in a different, more democratic direction. But we have to be honest. Things are *dire*. We are in a global political crisis. And simultaneously a global ecological crisis and a climate crisis. And unifying the two, we have the global capitalist crisis. And I think that a starting point for analysis has to come back to that trinity.

Anna Willow: Clearly, we can't afford to wear rose colored glasses at this point. That's not going to help. Both of you talked about the challenges that we need to overcome, but what about areas of opportunity? What can people like us do to begin moving toward a more positive next world?

Joel Wainwright: What is to be done? That is the eternal question. What do we do now? Perhaps this is going to sound like a total cop-out, but a huge part of what we're talking about is a crisis of understanding and imagination. David summed it up earlier when he said that the climate crisis is fundamentally a problem of democracy. If he is right, that means the first order of business is for us to reimagine democracy. To understand that what we have doesn't work and communicate it a thousand different ways through our lives. And to spin out of that process new forms of democratic existence and life that are adequate to the challenge of our political, ecological, and economic crises. That might sound kind of vague, but it's not. It comes down to the basic question of answering the questions—you might say existential, ontological problems—that we all face in our life. What is life for? If you find yourself—as we all do—living amidst a serious crisis like this, then what is life about? And how do we communicate the deep meaning of this crisis to the people around us in order to re-create and re-order our relationships so that they become seeds of a radically different world? I know that sounds abstract, but I think it means many different things to many different people, and I will leave it as a challenge for you to think about how to take it forward.

Anna Willow: That is our inspiration here at ROAR—the idea that we need to use our imaginations, work hard to open up possible channels, and do things that inspire us to put pieces of that next world into place. Let's turn those questions over to you, David. What do you, on the one hand, see as the biggest challenges we need to overcome and then, on the other hand, what are our greatest areas of opportunity? What can people like us do to create the positive next world we would love to see?

David Orr: Let me say three things. One is that there is no good reason for optimism. That's just not the reality at this point. The hard numbers are running against us. But there *is* every reason to be hopeful, creative, and dedicated to a better future. This is not an academic thing; this is our lives. The second thing I'll say is this: Americans have a problem thinking about this because for 40 years—your entire life if you're under that age—we've waged a war against government. We've heard, "Get government off our backs." It started in earnest with Ronald Reagan. Now if you follow the money, we see that a lot of people benefitted from less government surveillance, less law, less regulation. But they sold us a pig in a poke. They sold us a bill of goods. "Get government off your back" still leaves corporate power in place, and it can be as tyrannical as any government but without the restraints of law and democracy. Government and law keep our political conversations alive and contained. We will never resolve the tension between freedom and equality. The point is to keep those conversations going, to buy us time to learn more and see the human experience more broadly. The point is to keep the human experiment going as fairly and decently as possible. Of late, politics has become like a football game without rules and referees. Teams show up with R-15s and hand grenades. But that's not football, it's war.

…The third thing I'll say is that we need to uphold the standard of truth as best as humans can discern it. That means a commitment to data, facts, logic, evidence, and reason. Every fascist regime does two things: It wages a war on the existing government it attempts to overthrow and it creates an alternative reality, or as Kellyanne Conway (Senior Counselor to Donald Trump) put, it "alternative facts." As Patrick Moynihan said long ago, you're entitled to your opinion, but you're not entitled to your facts. The laws of gravity work regardless of your political opinion. And they become particularly important when you're in an airplane or standing on the edge of a tall building. The fight against law, facts, data, and evidence that we see playing out daily in American politics is simply to undermine our common sense of where we are, what we are, and what's true and false. If a regime can do that, they can undermine lots of other things. Let's look at the control of language. I started by saying that democracy requires a shift in thinking where "I, me, and mine" becomes "ours, we, and us." Finally, I'd like to say that if we invent this democracy that works, I hope it includes future generations. I hope it is an intergenerational democracy. They'll be a lot more of them—my grandkids, your children—than there are of us. And then let's widen the circle a little bit more to include the rights of other life forms to exist. Whether fungi, or elephants, or dolphins, or bears. Let's begin to assume that humans are not alone on this Earth, and that democracy needs to take into account the rights of other living creatures. Our future could be very violent, and a lot of people are going to fight for that smaller, meaner world. But a large majority favor a fair world. Clean air? Yes! Clear water? Yes! Stable climate? Yes! Justice, healthcare. A world in which the elderly do not live in poverty, the sick are afforded decent care, and the unemployed are provided opportunities to do good work.

Anna Willow: Getting a bit more technical, how do you think we can drawdown greenhouse gasses and become carbon neutral? What do you see as potential solutions? Carbon taxes? Something else?

David Orr: I think taxes are fairly reliable and you can determine what kind of response rates you will get. Cap and trade and other policy tools are less reliable in that sense, but they're more definitive in setting a limit on how much carbon you allow to enter the atmosphere. Frankly, the situation is so dire at this point, we must try many things. We must use the entire toolbox. But to return to our earlier discussion, this is not a technological or even an economic issue. It's a political leadership issue. But we are not without options. Every college in this country and every private school should aim to be solar powered and carbon neutral by 2030. Set the example. Begin the transition to electric vehicles or, even better, design a world where you don't need many vehicles at all. We have to try everything. Bikes. Wind power and solar.

Joel Wainwright: We tend to get bogged down on the technical details of what we could do here or there and on policy debates like carbon tax versus cap and trade. Let's just keep things simple. We've always known what we need to do to avoid catastrophic climate change. We have to stop taking fossil fuels out of the Earth's crust and burning them. It's really that simple. You have to stop the exploration and expansion of the mechanisms used to extract fossil fuels. There's a huge problem here, though, because the largest coal, oil, and natural gas companies in the world are, to generalize, the world's most powerful corporations, like ExxonMobil and Shell, or they are state capitalist enterprises, like we find in Russia, China, and Norway. And so, the technical question very quickly becomes a *political* question. It becomes a question of: Where will the power come from to take power away from those super-powerful states and corporations?

…This brings us right back to the problem of creating mass, democratic, transnational, trans-class movements to confront those forms of power. And then we face the capitalist organization of the political, where we face a paradox: On the one hand, climate change is a crisis of such grave proportions that we have no choice but to take it on in the existing horizon of the political, which is to say the existing terms of the capitalist nation-states. On the other hand, that system is totally set against distributing power democratically enough to take away the power of those who control, own, and exploit fossil fuels. That's the problem in a nutshell. To solve the puzzle of how to decarbonize global capitalism will mean addressing that paradox.

Anna Willow: At this point, do you believe that sustainable forms of economic development could work, or do we need to move toward degrowth and shift away from ideas of developing and growing our economies?

David Orr: Let's back up a little bit. We are—all of us—products of advertising. Studies suggest that each of us experiences something like 5,000 commercial advertisements every day. Let's assume that's an exaggeration. Let's cut it in half, so it's only 2,500. This is the largest attempt ever made in human history to deflect our consciousness. The way we think. You and I, everybody. To be good buyers. Dependable, dependent consumers of one thing or another. Our problem, as Joel points out, is partly a problem of ecological imagination. We're right in the middle of a global pandemic and what is capitalism selling us? Designer pet food and home cooked meals delivered to your door. Advertisements show us all kinds of amazing cars driving on roads with no other cars—and they're wonderful roads in California. They don't show you the burnt-out terrain in California caused by the combustion of fossil fuels and what comes out of the tailpipes of those same cars. This is what they have to sell us. The world is suffering and we're going through mass depression, we're told, around the United States and around the world because of rising COVID-19 cases and lockdowns. And what are they selling us? Gourmet dog food. More cars—the cause of the problem in the first place. It's like that old Rolling Stones line: "I can't get no satisfaction." There is no satisfaction and there is no curing these things until we deal with how our minds are being developed, whittled down, and shaped into what the advertisers want. Sustainable development has got to begin with a mind shift. A declaration of independence from that commercialized world that subverts our personalities, our souls, and our wellbeing.

Anna Willow: Your final thoughts, Joel?

Joel Wainwright: Let's be honest. To read the news these days is like picking up a trash can and dumping it on your head. It's overwhelming. The most important thing to hold onto and the thought I want to leave you with is that *you are not crazy*. If you look out at the world today and feel like things are really, deeply wrong, you are *right*. And if you feel that the opportunities availed to you in life—whether they include the products David just mentioned that you're supposed to buy in order to be happy, or what the political parties offer you, or the place in society that is already prepared for you as a worker/consumer—if these leave you feeling deeply unsettled, cause you anxiety, and you feel like things should be otherwise, you are *right*. So reject it!

But there are different ways to say "no." Best to reject it in a creative way where you cultivate imagination and critical understanding. And what is also crucial here is community, being in relationships with people you care about that allow you to have a dignified life of resistance within a world that is in the midst of some very serious problems. Without those forms of collective resistance feeding into forms of community, it simply cannot be sustained. I'm old enough to know that many of my friends who were very active in their 20s, if they weren't fortunate enough to build lives where their community fed into their activism and their activism fed into their community, one or the other fell away very quickly. They burned out, as we say. If you want to avoid burnout, you're going to have to solve a very specific puzzle, which is how to creatively build a life where forms of community reinforce participation in the cultivation of democratic acts of resistance. I wish you all the best in the process.

Where social and racial inequality come from today is deeply rooted in the infrastructures of society, whether that be police, our economics, redlining, political sectioning off. As we re-work the infrastructure, we will be able to fix those problems. And people will see that those problems still exist today, because a lot of people struggle to see that for what it is.

~George, 11th Grade

9

Our Converging Crises: COVID-19 and Climate Change

Climate change has recently been described as the "greatest existential crisis" humanity has ever faced (Chomsky et al. 2020:viii). It would be difficult to disagree with this assessment. After all, climate change comes with a long list of alarming consequences. As atmospheric concentrations of carbon dioxide and other greenhouse gasses climb, so does mean global temperature. As ice sheets and glaciers melt, sea levels rise. Coastal regions currently inhabited by millions of people will be inundated. Rapid biome shifts—coupled with habitat loss and other anthropogenic pressures—could cause the extinction of one third of all plant and animal species (Román-Palacios 2020). Oceans will continue to acidify as they absorb excess carbon dioxide, making life difficult for shellfish, corals, and those who rely on them. Extreme weather events—ranging from fires, droughts, and heat waves to unprecedented flooding and even cold snaps triggered by polar vortex destabilization—will become commonplace. And human health will suffer. Beyond the anguish associated with endless waves of (un)natural disasters, we will see declining crop yields and increasing food insecurity, the spread of infectious diseases, and decreased access to clean drinking water. Infrastructure and social systems not designed to endure will be strained to the point of collapse. Scarcity-driven conflicts and climate refugee crises will threaten national and international security.

The climate crisis is nothing if not newsworthy, but in some ways climate change is old news. The idea that anthropogenic releases of carbon dioxide could lead to global warming was proposed as early as the 1890s. For many decades, scientists alternately expressed concern about, debated, or ignored the proposition. By the mid-1980s, unambiguous evidence from ice cores showed that carbon dioxide concentrations and temperatures had risen and fallen together since the last ice age—and that both were surpassing the known maximums of historical records. Intentional efforts to undermine this evidence were propagated by the fossil fuel industry; eventually these seeds of doubt grew into full-fledged climate change denial, still endorsed by a dwindling but vocal minority (Weart 2011). By the turn of the millennium, it was widely accepted that the climate is changing and human activities are to blame. Environmental leaders around the world demanded action and governments answered...gradually. The 1997 Kyoto Protocol (which exempted poorer countries from climate action and which the United States refused to ratify) and 2009 Copenhagen Summit (which resulted in a weak statement rather than committed action) paved the way for the 2015 Paris Climate Agreement, the first binding international treaty designed to reduce greenhouse gas emissions and limit climate change and its effects. The Paris Agreement seeks to cap global temperature rise at a maximum of 2 degrees Celsius above the pre-industrial baseline—and at 1.5 degrees Celsius if at all possible—in order to evade climate change's most catastrophic effects.

Yet many worry that the Paris Agreement is a case of too little, too late. With atmospheric carbon dioxide concentrations now at 415 parts per million—far above the "safe" limit of 350 and still rising—we are already witnessing the damage climate change can do. 2020 brought the worst fire season on record to Australia and California. It brought devastating flooding to Mozambique and Bangladesh. With the ten hottest years on record all occurring since 2005, we are sailing into "planetary *terra incognita*, with an uncertain outcome in terms of the viability of contemporary civilization beyond this century or even the next few decades" (Steffen 2011:32). Global mean temperature has already risen by 1° Celsius above the pre-industrial baseline, with two-thirds of that warming occurring in the past four decades (IPCC 2018). The current trajectory has us heading toward a mean global temperature increase of 4 degrees Celsius by 2100. And it now appears that we will see severe ecological and social disruption even *if* the 1.5-degree target identified in the Paris Agreement is met (IPCC 2018; Steffen et al. 2018).

At this point, there is no way to fix, stop, or solve climate change. We cannot turn back time or magically restore the world we have lost. But neither are we doomed. We have a chance take action *now* to prevent a challenging situation from becoming catastrophic. Climate scientists tell us we have only a few years to dramatically reduce our emissions if we are to have a good chance of avoiding tipping points and thresholds that lock the Earth system into a set of mutually reinforcing feedbacks (e.g., permafrost and glacial melt, forest dieback) that end in a "hothouse earth" scenario (Steffen et al. 2018). What we do today, next week, and next year quite literally matters. We must cut global emissions in half by 2030 and then continue halving our emissions each decade thereafter until reaching net zero by 2050. Decisions made now, in this "critical decade," will influence the climate for hundreds if not thousands of years to come (Figueres and Rivett-Carnac 2020:xxii; see also Hansen et al. 2013).

Climate change is a problem so vast that it tests the limits of our comprehension. Its global extent, its long temporal frame, and its unfathomable impacts transcend anything we have experienced. And yet climate change does not stand alone. Since the Great Acceleration of the 1950s, economic activity, resource extraction, and other measures of consumption have risen dramatically along with measures of human impacts on the Earth's biogeophysical systems (ranging from forest loss and ocean dead zones to water impoundment and overfishing). The speed and scale of these changes has been astonishing. Within a single lifetime, humanity has become a dominant and destructive global force (Steffen 2015:94). Environmental decline and destabilization—of which climate change is the most significant part—now provide the context for our entire lives.

Confronting climate change becomes even more complicated—and more urgent—when we consider the fact that it is not at all fair. Who is responsible? Who should pay? And who should decide what happens next? Climate change is marked by an unfortunate irony: Since the days of the industrial revolution, the economically developed global North has built wealth and power by burning fossil fuels. In contrast, the economically undeveloped South contributed little (until quite recently) to the atmosphere's carbon dioxide concentration. But geography is cruel in this case; low latitudes will bear the brunt of the coming heat waves and droughts (Steffen 2011). Put simply, the nations that benefited from decades of conspicuous consumption stand to suffer comparatively little, while those that never enjoyed fossil-fueled prosperity stand to suffer the most. Indigenous peoples around the world also carry the burden of problems they did nothing to create, with many communities facing unprecedented threats to land-based resources and ways of life that have sustained them for generations (Figueroa 2011). Kiribati, Tuvalu, and other small island nations in the Pacific that rise only a few feet above the ocean will be the first to disappear beneath rising seas. The Arctic is another proverbial canary in the coalmine: Temperatures in the far north are rising faster than anywhere else in the world, making traditional subsistence increasingly difficult for Inuit communities (Nutall 2020; see also Crate and Nutall 2016). Alaskan Natives in Shishmaref and Newtok are already being forced to relocate as ocean waves wash away villages underlain by thawing permafrost (Marino 2015; Welch 2019).

Even within the world's wealthiest nations, low-income neighborhoods are more likely to be severely affected by climate change than higher-income ones. Poor people rarely enjoy "economic conditions that allow them to be resilient in climate hazards, nor can they often choose to leave their disadvantaged areas" (Robinson 2018:32). The climate justice movement addresses these inequities. Drawing inspiration from the broader environmental justice movement, which highlights the disproportionate environmental harms faced by poor and minority communities (Bullard 1990; Taylor 2014), climate justice advocates view climate change as yet "another example, or symptom, of social injustice" (Schlosberg and Collins 2014:363). They are united by their vehement critique of the unfair burdens of climate change and by the connections they make between the inequities of climate change and the long histories of colonialism and associated forms of injustice (Tokar 2020).

When we consider the causes of climate change and the causes of inequity within and between world regions, it quickly becomes apparent that the roots of these problems are tightly intertwined. Here too, climate change does not stand alone. The COVID-19 pandemic reminded us that health, food, energy, economy, education, justice, and environment are not only interconnected, but also that problems in one area almost always share origins with and have consequences in others. That our relationship to the planet we rely on is as broken as our relationships to one another indicates that a culture that condones extractivism and rewards self-centered-short-term thinking may be the biggest crisis of all. We have hard work ahead of us. Increasingly, we are coming to understand that our conjoined crises will only be resolved successfully and durably when they are resolved together. We don't just need new renewable energy and clean transportation technology, we need a whole new set of values, a whole new way of life.

In early 2020, schooling, transportation, and major sectors of the economy came to a grinding halt as lockdowns were imposed. With all but the most essential workers sent home and few options for entertainment, many people found their schedules forcibly cleared. Alone in our rooms, we pondered our prospects as never before. Yet even as the pandemic raged, many among us were well aware that climate change would ultimately wreak much greater havoc than COVID-19. People were dying, healthcare and food systems were strained to the point of collapse. But we knew what we were witnessing was nothing compared to the disruption climate change could soon bring. The pandemic offered a preview of the future, a mock laboratory "where the time scale of unfolding events is reduced from decades to days" (Fuentes et al. 2020:1). What, if anything, did we learn? Hopefully, we learned to attend to long-term trends, anticipate and mitigate inequities, and prepare proactively for impending challenges (Manzanedo and Manning 2020).

More specifically, we learned that shutting down the economy is neither necessary nor sufficient for long-term emissions reduction. When emissions plummeted early in the pandemic, there was hope that putting the world on hold might make a real difference in our climate change trajectory. Despite the momentary clear skies, however, this silver lining never materialized. While the effects of the pandemic itself on emissions appears negligible, the possibility of a green recovery holds considerable promise. Because our timeline to act is so short, the shape that COVID-19 recovery takes will have a significant influence on the future climate. Follow our current fossil-fueled trajectory and we are almost certain to exceed the 1.5-degree threshold by 2050. Implement a green recovery that incorporates strong climate policies and energy transition stimulus and we have a good chance at remaining below it (Forster et al. 2020). Instead of enforcing closures, we now recognize that climate action will require "much deeper social change coupled with a green transformation that decouples economic activity and carbon emissions" (Fuentes et al. 2020:9).

These are among the complex connections between COVID-19 and climate change taken up during our final Next World Conversation, held on January 7, 2021. We were joined by two inspiring guests: Alyssa Battistoni was an Environmental Fellow at Harvard University and co-author of *A Planet to Win: Why We Need a Green New Deal.* Reed Kurtz is a political scientist currently based at Purdue University. Our conversation also touched on what could turn out to be the most vital lesson of COVID-19. The pandemic taught us that we can live our lives in radically different ways. At both individual and collective levels, we are capable of changing our behavior. We can change not only how we work and where we spend our time, but also our broader societal expectations and arrangements. Knowing that we can live differently invites new visions of the future. As Christina Figueres (one of the Paris Agreement's lead architects) and Tom Rivett-Carnac tell us, "meeting the challenge of climate change needs to become part of a new story of human striving and renewal…When the story changes, everything changes" (2020:158). It is up to us to rewrite our story.

Anna Willow: I know both of you have a lot to say about the question I'm about to ask, but I'll start with Alyssa. As you see it, what is the relationship between COVID-19 and the climate crisis?

Alyssa Battistoni: I think that's a really interesting question because there are a few different ways to think about the covid/climate relationship. One is a very literal relationship in that as we see the climate changing, we are likely to see the emergence of new infectious diseases. Climate change causes organisms to move to new places, which leads to encounters between different kinds of living things. So we are going to have disease outbreaks, potentially including pandemics. At a deeper level, another relationship is that COVID-19 and the climate crisis are both caused by underlying patterns of capitalism in general and of industrial agriculture more specifically. We know that covid emerged out of the expanding urban interface, as people move into areas that used to be wild. In these cases, we encounter animals we aren't usually in contact with as well as diseases we may not have encountered before. But new diseases also emerge from industrial agriculture because it is such an intensive form of animal production and generates various forms of disease. Industrial agriculture is also a major contributor to climate change. So it's a complex and mutually reinforcing system, with climate change giving rise to new patterns of animal migration that produce not only new diseases but also new forms of animal production that produce both pandemics and climate change.

…An additional way we might think about the relationship between COVID-19 and the climate crisis has to do with our responses. Early on in the pandemic, there was a lot of discussion about the big reductions in emissions and pollution that resulted from quarantine and shutdown. There was also some discourse around wildlife returning to areas usually used by humans. These conversations spoke to the idea that we were drastically changing our behavior and our economic patterns. Suddenly, the state was stepping in and saying, "We're going shut some things down because they pose a serious threat to human life." That is not something that has happened on this scale in many people's lifetimes. So that was an interesting moment, and a lot of people wondered: If this can happen for a pandemic, why can't we do something like this for climate? We know we need to shut down or transition away from certain industries in order to avert a serious climate catastrophe, which is already upon us, so why can't we do it? There was a sense that the response to COVID-19 suggested that more is possible. It shows that we can take serious action to protect human and, I would say, non-human life. But as the pandemic has worn on, we've also seen the importance of resistance to economic shutdown and quarantine, particularly when it occurs without income support that allows people to get by in the absence of their usual job. It revealed both the possibilities and the things we need to figure out, like how to sustain people through a transitional moment, the challenges of shutting down economic activity without providing alternatives, and the kind of backlash that can occur. I'm actually very worried that the response to covid in the US foretells what we're likely to see in response to climate action; the idea that the cure is worse than the disease. If certain industries are shut down without offering people a just transition—without actually giving people alternatives—I think many people will reject and react against the economic intervention we know is needed to tackle climate change. One last connection between COVID-19 and climate change is their very uneven effects. We've seen this with covid and we're already seeing it with climate change in the case of every disaster. It reveals and exacerbates existing social inequalities.

Anna Willow: It's amazing that at both the causal and the consequential levels, looking at covid requires looking at almost every dimension of our lives. Reed, what is your take on the relationship between COVID-19 and the climate crisis?

Reed Kurtz: I tend to think about the relationship a bit more abstractly. For me, there are two main implications of thinking about covid and the climate crisis together. The first is to recognize their intertwined nature and the ways in which 21st century crises are profoundly interconnected. These crises' repercussions extend far beyond our ability to measure their immediate geographical and temporal contexts. When it comes to climate change, the effects are going to be generational. The same can be said for covid, insofar as we do not know what the long-term effects will be. Not only are the biological impacts of carrying the disease uncertain, but we also don't know what the psychological, social, and emotional effects on an entire generation might be. For better or worse, this is a generation-defining moment. We are living through an event in human history that is unprecedented in many ways…which returns me to considering climate and covid not alone but as part of a broader crisis of crises. We might think of it as the planetary ecological crisis. Some people call it the Anthropocene to reflect the idea that human activity is transforming the planet on a geological scale that is literally unprecedented in the history of the planet. I prefer to think of it in terms of the *capitalocene*, or the age of capital. Our planet's transformations are defined by a capitalist system that is both the backdrop and the cause of the massive drama that is now unfolding. And it's not only creating the problems, but it's also shaping and limiting our alternatives and possibilities. One thing this pandemic has highlighted is the fact that issues in this country and around the world are profoundly intertwined. We cannot understand the effects covid is having on people without understanding racial, sexual, and economic differences and divisions. Understanding covid and climate change as part of a broader ecological crisis is necessary not only for understanding the sources and origins of the crises we're facing, but also for understanding their resolutions. Tackling these problems cannot be done with piecemeal approaches that look at economic issues as if they were separate from social welfare, or think of racial justice as disconnected from demands for a living wage or better working conditions and a better, cleaner environment. We have to see these issues as intertwined both to understand what has happened and to conceptualize what solutions will look like.

...A second major implication concerns the strategic political consequences and contexts that these events produce for us. We have to be asking ourselves: What does this mean strategically for the goals we seek? If we are seeking economic, social, and climate justice, what does the current context bode? I pose that as an open question. If the past year—and maybe even the past four years—have taught us anything, it is the profound inability of our political system and institutions to deal with these crises in an equitable, just, responsible, and effective manner. It should be evident to all of us that the US government has utterly failed to manage this crisis—and I'm referring to both the covid crisis and the climate crisis—in a way that produces anything resembling a just and sustainable resolution. Which begs the question: If our political institutions have proven themselves incapable over and over and failed systematically and consistently, then what is to be done? This is the classic revolutionary question. What is to be done? A Green New Deal is definitely part of the equation, but we also need to be asking what political institutional system is necessary for devising and implementing solutions as well as for opening horizons and possibilities. And this raises bigger questions about whether or not the US state apparatus— the US government as we understand it—is capable of responding to these crises. For the record, I would wager that as it stands right now, the US state apparatus and the global capitalist system are incapable of responding to either the climate crisis or the covid crisis in a fair, just, equitable, and sustainable manner. We have seen it time and time again. This crisis has only proven it. Even in the countries that have responded well, we have to demand more if we're going to take on climate change.

Anna Willow: I also have a specific question for you, Reed. In the introduction to the special issue you recently co-edited for the journal *Radical Philosophy Review*, you pose an important question: Is the pandemic a setback in the struggle against climate change or is it a springboard?[12]

Reed Kurtz: I think that is still to be determined. Ultimately, the question of whether covid presents an opportunity or a setback is a political question, which means that it will be determined politically, through the struggles of exercising power and through the production of consensual agreement, but also through the exercise of coercive force if necessary. I agree with Alyssa that we need to be very, very cautious about any victory we claim or any optimism we sustain. The reality is that many worrying tendencies have emerged out of this crisis.

Anna Willow: "What is to be done?" is an important question. The past several years have been frustrating—even aside from the pandemic. One thing I've realized is that government won't save us and business won't save us. We have to do it ourselves. As I see it, this lesson could be one of the most important gifts we can give to the next generation. And, honestly, that's what we are here to do, where the inspiration for our Next World Conversations came from. The idea that we need to make change in our communities and spread positive change rhizomatically has been really encouraging and empowering. Alyssa, would you like to weigh in on whether you see covid as a setback or a springboard for climate action before we move on?

Alyssa Battistoni: I agree with Reed that it's too soon to tell. I would guess it is both, but to what degree and what we'll look back and see is still unknown. What I do know is that the repercussions of this are huge, both the death and illness the pandemic has caused and the economic

---

[12] See Kurtz, Reed M., and Harry van der Linden. 2020. Radical Philosophy and Politics Amid the Climate Crisis and the Coronavirus Pandemic. *Radical Philosophy Review* 23(2):161-174.

toll. We have a k-shaped recovery, where people who have stocks or jobs they can do from home are doing fine. They have more savings than ever. But people who work in low wage jobs are completely out of luck. We'll see repercussions of this for a very long time to come. That said, I'm very worried right now. The Black Lives Matter protests over the summer [of 2020] were not about covid specifically, but the outsize toll that the pandemic has taken on Black people in the country is hard to separate from police brutality against Black people. And the economic toll on people who are essential workers, but who are not treated or paid as if they're essential, is also among the multitudinous forces that went into those moments of uprising and protest. But that is really the one bright spot of resistance, of demanding more, over the course of this year. The rest of it feels like a lot of setbacks to me. It's sort of shocking to realize how many people have died and see that there hasn't been a mass movement in response. I don't know what it would look like in this instance, but I feel like people should have been protesting. A pandemic is a very demobilizing event. It's very isolating. It takes people away from each other. It's antisocial. All of these things. And to the extent that people have been gathering, it's largely been on the political right. I think there may be a lot of pent-up anger and, as Reed said, it's very hard to look at the US government and think that it's functional, that it's working for people, that we can trust it to have our interests at heart. I think a lot of this has been laid bare, especially with the economy so clearly prioritized above people's lives. There will be some things that will be hard to unsee. But, speaking as someone on the political left, we don't have the power we need to have. This has been a moment of crisis, which is supposedly an opportunity. But it has not been an opportunity we have been able to seize, and that is very concerning to me.

Anna Willow: I didn't consider myself an optimist for most of my life. But I have to believe that the sort of latent movement you hinted at is building, and that gives me hope. People might not be out in the streets, but I can tell they are thinking and preparing themselves mentally. With that in mind, I'd like both of you to dream big for a few minutes. How *could* we be responding to the climate crisis and the other crises that are entwined with it? If there were no limitations, what would you like to see happen?

Reed Kurtz: One positive outcome of the covid crisis is that it has forced us to reckon with the world in ways we have never done before. Literally. We have had to rethink everything about how we organize our lives, about how we organize society. It is true that we have failed thus far to seize the opportunity at hand. But I also sense a lot of latent energy and unspent potential. In terms of our response to climate change, we know this decade is absolutely critical. The science tells us that we must reduce global net greenhouse gas emissions by 50 percent within the next decade if we are to have a chance at a remotely just and sustainable future. That gives us a sense of what we're dealing with. It also gives us a sense of what we need to do. It is alarmingly clear that we do not have a decade to implement a Green New Deal. It must be implemented as soon as possible.

…So what concrete steps do we need to take? Starting yesterday, there has to be legal accountability for the people who have been running this country and tearing it apart from the top down. If we don't do that, I don't know how we can achieve any of our other goals. Following that, we also have to implement a Green New Deal. We have to get it going. It has to be a radical Green New Deal, one that is just, fair, and equitable. One that empowers workers and does not divide the working class. There are debates going on right now about what that might look like. Again, though, I have to insist that we do not have a decade for a Green New Deal. We have a ticking clock and every day we postpone means the stakes are magnified. Once we get beyond that, we will need a political imagination. We need a horizon of political possibility that extends beyond what we are capable of envisioning right now. The planet operates on cycles that are much longer than our two or four-year electoral cycles. This means that we have to be thinking beyond the current system. We have to be thinking: What would a just and equitable alternative to capitalism look like? What would an ecological society that is not ruled by the capitalist class and does not put the economy over human life look like? What are the origins of such a society? And what are the obstacles to achieving it? We also need to ask real questions about whether the political institutions in this country are capable of implementing the decarbonization that is necessary in the timeframe that is necessary. We need to raise questions about a nation-state founded upon settler colonialism, white supremacy, and a conception of nature as endlessly bountiful and exploitable. And, finally, we need to think about what a more democratic and ecologically sustainable organization of political relationships would look like. This might mean rewriting the US constitution. There are cases where this kind of thing has been done democratically. Private property and corporate management of our economy are written into our constitution. So if we're unable or unwilling to raise questions that strike at the heart of the American nation-state, we have to ask ourselves if we are capable of tackling this crisis or not. It's very important that we think beyond the constraints of what a capitalist society or even a Green New Deal could provide. We need to be thinking about what a post-capitalist world would look like. We need to be thinking about how we could reorganize social and ecological relations in a more democratic manner. We need democracy inside the household. We need democracy inside the workplace. And we need democracy inside the institutions that govern and regulate our society. If we are unable to strike at the heart of the capitalist system that is destroying this planet and destroying lives, then we will fail. That is just how it is.

Anna Willow: It's your turn, Alyssa. In your view, how should we be responding to the climate crisis?

Alyssa Battistoni: I agree with Reed about the need to completely rethink our economy and systems of government. We need to think about a world beyond capitalism. But in the more immediate term, I see the Green New Deal as buying time for a longer-term project of broader social and economic transformation. This transformation is absolutely imperative, but I don't think it's going to happen this decade. I could be wrong. But, for me, the Green New Deal is a start. It's not a one-and-done piece of legislation; it's an ongoing project. I think we're in the *generation* of the Green New Deal. How do we start building the society we want to see in the long-term *now*, in the present? How do we begin to decarbonize today and also build power for future transformations? Obviously, as Reed said, we have to start right now.

…There are a lot of things I would like to do in the immediate term. I will talk about one of them now. One thing that frustrated me over the course of the pandemic was our failure to kick the oil industry while it was down. Oil prices dropped dramatically this year because demand was way down and there was a price war between Russia and the Saudis. American oil production is uneconomic; it's not profitable when oil prices are low because of the amount of capital invested in fracking. Quite a few smaller-scale operators declared bankruptcy this year. A hundred thousand oil and gas workers were—or still are—out of work. So it was a great opportunity to nationalize the oil and gas industry; a great time to buy out oil and gas shares cheaply, put the industry on a managed decline, and transition workers to other jobs. We also need to do many other things. We need to build clean energy, public transportation, and housing. We could get started on these things right now. But we absolutely have to stop using fossil fuels.

…We have a chance to engage people who have lost jobs and kickstart the just transition. We can create non-destructive jobs for people who have lost work or will lose work because of the shutdown of their world-destroying industries. This way, workers don't have to go down with the ship or pay for the decisions their bosses made. Green jobs—and even a green job guarantee—have been talked about for a long time. This would be a great time to do it. But you need a proof of concept, so you can say, "I know you've heard a lot about green jobs. Here is the green job. You lost your job because the oil industry is crashing, not because of climate action. And because it's a very volatile industry." Right now, we can show people that green jobs are not just an idea but can also be real and concrete. We can win people's support. In terms of other things we should be doing, we could be spending the stimulus money associated with covid relief on things that would help instantiate parts of the Green New Deal right away. Both stimulus packages passed in 2020 are much larger than anything we could have imagined a year ago. So the money is there. What we need to be doing with that money is laying the groundwork *not* for going back to normal—because normal is not great, and normal is getting worse and worse—but for moving toward a different future.

Anna Willow: We've already talked about some wonderful opportunities, but I'd like to also consider our limitations. In your view, Alyssa, what are our biggest challenges? What is preventing us from making these changes?

Alyssa Battistoni: Even now, fossil capital remains very powerful. More generally, capital remains very powerful. We also have some serious political challenges. As Reed said, the political system is completely dysfunctional right now. So even with people who say they want to do something about climate change taking charge, it's hard to see a large climate-oriented spending package. Sometimes it feels like you need to have a revolution or a massive movement to achieve basic reform in this country. If the Green New Deal is the reform, but you need a revolutionary movement to achieve it, that is a paradox.

Anna Willow: Reed, what do you think? What are our biggest challenges? Our greatest opportunities?

Reed Kurtz: One of the biggest challenges we face is the hegemony of fossil capitalism, which has both an ideological dimension and a very profound material dimension. We see it ideologically in that our understandings of how life is and could be are profoundly shaped and limited by the fossil-fueled society we live in. In a country like the United States, people's identities are shaped by their connection to motorsports or to their wants and consumption habits. This presents a huge challenge when we think about how to create a more equal, sustainable, and just society for all. The material dimension is also very important, which gets at what Alyssa was saying about essential workers and how economic conditions compel people to put themselves at risk. Right now, the other challenge we face is getting people on board. In polls immediately after the November 3, 2020 election, approximately 50 percent of voters said President Trump handled the COVID-19 crisis either "somewhat well" or "very well." This is extraordinary when we consider how bungled the response was. And so, we really need to think about how to get the segment of the population with this ideological leaning on board with the changes that are needed to tackle climate change.

Anna Willow: Do you think it will ever be possible to shift the government's focus from economic gain to environmental concerns, given the number of people in our society who seem to oppose sustainability? Could we shift our collective values?

Alyssa Battistoni: In a way, that is *the* question. There are competing functions of the state: One is to be a provider of services, and in that way, it is nominally responsible to democratic demands of the people. While we can be quite cynical about that, we shouldn't throw it out the window. The problem is that so much is tethered to economic gain, economic growth, and the needs of capital. At some point, though, we have to reorient both what we think of as economic gains and what the government is for.

Reed Kurtz: We need to be thinking very concretely about where the reproduction of society occurs. The social reproduction of capitalism does not simply take place inside of factories or on the assembly line. It's not just the relationship of the worker to the boss. It's broader than that, which means there are far more arenas of struggle available. Nurses, healthcare workers, teachers—all of these people are workers who are instrumental in the reproduction of capitalism as a social and ecological system. We need a broader and more expansive conception of what labor is and could be that is not constrained by the demand for endless exploitation and reproduction of the capitalist system. I would suggest we start there. How could we have more just and equitable relations within our households, within our workplaces, within our schools, and within our society at large? And so, thinking concretely, what can we do? We have to organize. We need to undertake collective action. We need to democratize all aspects of society, at all scales.

---

*There's no one solution to climate change.
There are a thousand different potential
opportunities to fix specific problems.*
~John, 10th Grade

10
Your Turn:
A Workbook For Change

This volume does not have a conclusion, because this is not the end. We hope that the ideas shared here inspire action in communities near and far. We hope that these Next World Conversations provide good places to start making change and (more importantly) give readers the sense that change is possible. We began this project with the goal of collecting and presenting new visions of positive futures, alternative worlds worth striving for. While our conversation series has reached its end, the authors—accompanied by others involved in Regional Ohio Action for Resilience—continue spend each day building stronger, healthier, more sustainable, and more equitable communities. Our journey is multigenerational; our work has no end in sight. But this final chapter is not about us. The next Next World Conversations belong to you. What changes would you like to see? How will you catalyze them? Where will you begin?

In the pages that follow, you will find a workbook designed to inspire visions of what your own next world might look like and empower you to start putting pieces of that next world into place. This workbook draws on *visioning* (creating a positive image of the future) and *backcasting* (visioning a desirable future and then projecting backward to deduce how it came to be) techniques that are widely utilized within the Transition movement (see chapter 2) to motivate participants and organize ambitions (Hopkins 2008, 2011). Regardless of whether you are experienced in the work of social change or just taking your first steps, the exercises in this workbook will be a useful tool and should be adapted to meet your own needs. While spaces to write or draw are included, you may choose to collect your ideas in another creative way. You may opt to respond to the prompts alone or in a group, in a meditative space or a celebratory one. Reading groups may wish to combine these options, with individuals completing exercises independently and regrouping to share and strategize. The timeframe you choose to envision is also up to you. While we suggest envisioning the world in 20 to 30 years' time, you may find a shorter or longer increment more useful. Whatever strategy you select, you will not walk alone. You will be joined by concerned citizens in thousands of communities around the world who are working tirelessly to put a positive next world within reach. This isn't the end. It's a new beginning. We invite you to join us as we reclaim the future, one community at a time.

Close your eyes for a few moments and allow yourself to mentally step into the future. Let your creativity flow and engage your senses so that this world feels as real as possible. It is a positive future in which we have managed to overcome fossil fuel addiction and are adapting successfully to a changed climate. It doesn't have to be a utopia, and you are not expected to have fully-formulated ideas. Your job is simply to brainstorm what life in your future community is like.

I am envisioning the **year**:

In the **community** of:

1) What stands out about your vision? What are the most exciting aspects of the future you imagine? Write or draw your ideas!

Now you are ready to think more deeply about some of the specific elements of the future you envision. How do people meet their needs and use the earth's resources? How do they interact with others and pass their time? What matters most in this future world?

2) Think about water in your community of the future. Where is water and what roles does it play? How do people access fresh, clean water?

3) How do you envision the future of food in your community? What do people eat? And where does it come from?

4) What is the future of waste in your community? What kinds of waste do people produce and where does it go?

5) Envision the future of energy in your community. How do you and other community members generate and access electricity and other forms of power?

6) How would you describe the future economy of your community? What do you do for your job? What do others do?

7) How do you envision the future of transportation in your community? How do people travel from place to place?

8) What does the built and natural environment look and feel like? Where do you and other residents of the future live, work, learn, pray, and play? Write or draw your ideas!

9) What key values are expressed in your vision of the future? What do people in the next world care about?

10) What do you and other residents of the future do for fun?

It's time to come back to the present. It is important to think about your community's unique circumstances and select the areas you would like to work on first. Prioritizing is not about attending to some issues and disregarding others. It is about giving yourself a manageable place to start. Trust that work in other areas will follow.

11) What key challenges does your community face?

12) What assets, resources, and ongoing projects exist in your community? What positive things are already happening?

13) Think or look back to your visions of the future. Where is your work most needed? Where will it be most effective? Pick one or two priorities to help you focus your efforts.

Now, it's time to *backcast*. This will help you determine the steps that will take you from your current reality to the positive future you would like to see. Be strategic and consider when the structures that will support the future you envision need to be in place. It may be helpful to create a timeline that begins today and leads up to your selected date.

14) Think about the priority area/s you selected. How will the future you envision become reality?

15) Identify one change you can make right now that will take you in your desired direction:

16) Commit to making changes in your priority areas. What will you do this week? This month? This year?

This week I will:

This month I will:

This year I will:

I imagine a city that is not polluted. You would be able to live in a place that is urban and natural at the same time. You would have public transport and green spaces and clean air and water. And everything would be designed in a way that is sustainable and functional, but still urban enough to support a growing population...a society where everyone has a deeper connection with nature and can go outside more.

~Ella, 11th Grade

I'd love to be able to have a world where I can go outside and see more than three stars at night.

~John, 10th Grade

Instead of spending your money to acquire material things, we would have a world and an economy where we can focus on our community and interactions. Everyone would have an active role in the community.

~George, 11th Grade

References and Resources

Agyeman, Julian, David Schlosberg, Luke Craven, and Caitlin Matthews. 2016. Trends and Directions in Environmental Justice: From Inequity to Everyday Life, Community, and Just Sustainabilites. *Annual Review of Environment and Resources* 41:321-340.

Alkon, Alison Hope and Julian Agyeman. 2011. Introduction: The Food Movement as Polyculture. In *Cultivating Food Justice: Race, Class, and Sustainability*, edited by Alison Hope Alkon and Julian Agyeman. Pp. 1-20. Boston: The MIT Press.

Alexander, Samuel, and Brendan Gleeson. 2019. *Degrowth in the Suburbs: A Radical Urban Imaginary.* Singapore: Palgrave Macmillan.

American Forests. No date. Tree Equity in America's Cities. https://www.americanforests.org/our-work/urban-forestry (accessed August 15, 2021).

Anderson, Ben. 2006. "Transcending Without Transcendence": Utopianism and an Ethos of Hope. *Antipode* 38(4):691-710.

Anderson, E.N. 2010. *The Pursuit of Ecotopia: Lessons from Indigenous and Traditional Societies for the Human Ecology of Our Modern World.* Santa Barbara, California: Praeger.

Aronoff, Kate, Alyssa Battistoni, Daniel Aldana Cohen, and Thea Riofrancos. 2019. *A Planet to Win: Why We Need a Green New Deal.* London: Verso Books.

Badger, Emily. 2021. A Little Remote Work Could Change Rush Hour a Lot. *New York Times*, June 11, 2021. https://www.nytimes.com/2021/06/11/upshot/rush-hour-remote-work.html (accessed July 12, 2021).

Belli, Brita. 2020. Racial Disparity in Police Shootings Unchanged Over 5 Years. *YaleNews*, October 27, 2020. https://news.yale.edu/2020/

10/27/racial-disparity-police-shootings-unchanged-over-5-years (accessed July 29, 2021).

Berry, Wendell. 1977. *The Unsettling of America: Culture and Agriculture.* San Francisco: Sierra Club Books.

Biddau, Fulvio, Alessandra Armenti, and Paolo Cottone. 2016. Socio-Psychological Aspects of Grassroots Participation in the Transition Movement: An Italian Case Study. *Journal of Social and Political Psychology* 4(1):142-165.

Bischoff, Laura. 2020. Fight Over Controversial Energy Bailout Law Delayed in Ohio House. *Dayton Daily News*, October 26, 2020. https://www.daytondailynews.com/news/fight-over-energy-bailout-law-delayed/N22TP5LW75BFBILCQ7QM2GLRWU/ (accessed July 13, 2021).

Boyer, Robert. 2016. Achieving One-Planet Living Through Transitions in Social Practice: A Case Study of Dancing Rabbit Ecovillage. *Sustainability: Science, Practice and Policy* 12(1):47-59.

Brand, Ulrich, and Marian Lang. 2019. Green Economy. In *Pluriverse: A Post-Development Dictionary*, edited by Ashish Kithari, Ariel Selleh, Arturo Escobar, Federico Demaria, and Alberto Acosta. Pp. 56-59. New Delhi, India: Tulika Books.

Brooks, David. 2020. The Future of American Politics. *New York Times*, January 30, 2020. https://www.nytimes.com/2020/01/30/opinion/us-politics.html (accessed January 18, 2022).

Brooks, David. 2021. How Racist Is America? *New York Times*, July 22, 2021. https://www.nytimes.com/2021/07/22/opinion/how-racist-is-america.html (accessed August 10, 2021).

Brown, Susan Love. 2002a. Introduction. In *Intentional Community: An Anthropological Perspective*, edited by Susan Love Brown. Pp. 1-15. Albany: State University of New York Press.

Brown, Susan Love. 2002b. Community as Cultural Critique. In *Intentional Community: An Anthropological Perspective*, edited by

Susan Love Brown. Pp. 153-179. Albany: State University of New York Press.

Bruner, Edward M. 1986. Ethnography as Narrative. In *The Ethnography of Experience*, edited by Victor W. Turner and Edward M. Bruner, pp. 139-155. Urbana: University of Illinois Press.

Bullard, Robert D. 1990. *Dumping in Dixie: Race, Class, and Environmental Quality.* Boulder, Colorado: Westview Press.

Burke, Brian J., and Beatriz Arjona. 2013. Creating Alternative Political Ecologies through the Construction of Ecovillages in Colombia. In *Environmental Anthropology Engaging Ecotopia: Bioregionalism, Permaculture, and Ecovillages,* edited by Joshua Lockyer and James R. Veteto. Pp. 235-250. New York: Berghahn Books.

Cajete, Gregory. 1994. *Look to the Mountain: An Ecology of Indigenous Education.* Durango, Colorado: Kivaki Press.

Cammarota, Julio, and Michelle Fine. 2008. Youth Participatory Action Research: A Pedagogy for Transformational Resistance. In *Revolutionizing Education: Youth Participatory Action Research in Motion*, edited by Julio Cammarota and Michelle Fine. Pp. 1-11. New York: Routledge.

Carlsson, Chris. 2008. *Nowtopia: How Pirate Programmers, Outlaw Bicyclists, and Vacant-Lot Gardeners are Inventing the Future Today.* Oakland, California: AK Press.

Carlsson, Chris, and Francesca Manning. 2010. Nowtopia: Strategies Exodus? *Antipode* 42(4):924-953.

Carspecken, Lucinda. 2012. *An Unreal Estate: Sustainability and Freedom in an Evolving Community.* Bloomington: Indiana University Press.

Ceballos, Gerardo, Paul R. Ehrlich, and Peter H. Raven. 2020. Vertebrates on the Brink as Indicators of Biological Annihilation and the Sixth Mass Extinction. *Proceedings of the National Academy of Sciences* 117(24):13596-13602.

Chandler, Adam. 2016. Where the Poor Spend More Than 10 Percent of their Income on Energy. *The Atlantic*, June 8, 2016. https://www.theatlantic.com /business/archive/2016/06/energy-poverty-low-income-households/486197/ (accessed June 25, 2021).

Chapin, F. Stuart, Mary E. Power, Steward T.A. Pickett, Amy Freitag, Julie A. Reynolds, Robert B. Jackson, David M. Lodge, et al. 2011. Earth Stewardship: Science for Action to Sustain the Human-Earth System. *Ecosphere* 2(8):1-20.

Chomsky, Noam, Robert Pollin, and C. J. Polychroniou. 2020. *Climate Crisis and the Global Green New Deal: The Political Economy of Saving the Planet.* London: Verso.

Chuli, Mónica, Grimaldo Rengifo, and Eduardo Gudynas. 2019. Buen Vivir. In *Pluriverse: A Post-Development Dictionary*, edited by Ashish Kithari, Ariel Selleh, Arturo Escobar, Federico Demaria, and Alberto Acosta. Pp. 111-114. New Delhi, India: Tulika Books.

Collins, Samuel Gerald. 2007. *All Tomorrow's Cultures: Anthropological Engagements with the Future.* New York: Berghahn Books.

Costanza, Robert, Ida Kubiszewski, Enrico Giovannini, Hunter Lovins, Jacqueline McGlade, Kate E. Pickett, Kristín Vala Ragnarsdóttir, Debra Roberts, Roberto De Vogli, and Richard Wilkinson. 2014. Development: Time to Leave GDP behind. *Nature News* 505(7483):283-285.

Crate, Susan A., and Mark Nuttall, eds. 2016. *Anthropology and Climate Change: From Encounters to Actions.* New York: Routledge.

Cronon, William. 1995. The Trouble with Wilderness; or, Getting Back to the Wrong Nature. In *Uncommon Ground: Rethinking the Human Place in Nature,* edited by William Cronon. Pp. 69-90. New York: W.W. Norton and Company.

Curtin, Sally C. 2020. State Suicide Rates Among Adolescents and Young Adults Aged 10–24: United States, 2000–2018. *National Vital Statistics Reports* 69(11):1-9.

D'Amato, Dalia, Nils Droste, Ben Allen, Marianne Kettunen, Katja Lähtinen, Jaana Korhonen, Pekka Leskinen, Brent D. Matthies, and Anne Toppinen. 2017. Green, Circular, Bio Economy: A Comparative Analysis of Sustainability Avenues. *Journal of Cleaner Production* 168:716-734.

Degrowth. 2020. The Birth of the Degrowth Movement: A Map, a Meeting and a Dream. https://www.degrowth.info/en/map/ (accessed November 4, 2020).

Demaria, Federíco, and Serge Latouche. 2019. Degrowth. In *Pluriverse: A Post-Development Dictionary*, edited by Ashish Kithari, Ariel Selleh, Arturo Escobar, Federico Demaria, and Alberto Acosta. Pp. 148-151. New Delhi, India: Tulika Books.

Demaria, Federico, Francois Schneider, Filka Sekulova, and Joan Martinez-Alier. 2013. What is Degrowth? From an Activist Slogan to a Social Movement. *Environmental Values* 22(2):191-215.

Demaria, Federico, Giorgos Kallis, and Karen Bakker. 2019. Geographies of Degrowth: Nowtopias, Resurgences and the Decolonization of Imaginaries and Places. *Environment and Planning E: Nature and Space* 2(3):431-450.

Dewey, John. 1986 [1938]. Experience and Education. *The Educational Forum* 50(3):241-252.

Díaz, Sandra, Josef Settele, and Eduardo Brondízio, et al. 2019. *Summary for Policymakers of the Global Assessment Report on Biodiversity and Ecosystem Services of the Intergovernmental Science-Policy Platform on Biodiversity and Ecosystem Services.* Intergovernmental Science-Policy Platform on Biodiversity and Ecosystem Services (IPBES). https://www.ipbes.net/news/Media-Release-Global-Assessment (accessed May 24, 2019).

The Economist. Greenhouse Gas Emissions are Set to Rise Fast in 2021. *The Economist*, April 20, 2021. https://www.economist.com/graphic-detail/2021/04/20/greenhouse-gas-emissions-are-set-to-rise-fast-in-2021 (accessed August 2, 2021).

Eligon, John, and Shawn Hubler. 2021. Throughout Trial Over George Floyd's Death, Killings by Police Mount. *New York Times*, April 17, 2021. https://www.nytimes.com/2021/04/17/us/police-shootings-killings.html (accessed July 10, 2021).

Escobar, Laura Gutiérrez. 2019. Food Sovereignty. In *Pluriverse: A Post-Development Dictionary*, edited by Ashish Kithari, Ariel Selleh, Arturo Escobar, Federico Demaria, and Alberto Acosta. Pp. 185-188. New Delhi, India: Tulika Books.

Fairchild, Denise. 2017. Conclusion: Building an Energy Democracy Movement. In *Energy Democracy: Advancing Equity in Clean Energy Solutions*, edited by Denise Fairchild and Al Weinrub. Pp. 239-250. Washington, DC: Island Press.

Felicetti, Andrea. 2017. *Deliberative Democracy and Social Movements: Transition Initiatives in the Public Sphere*. New York: Rowman and Littlefield.

Figueres, Christiana, and Tom Rivett-Carnac. 2020. *The Future We Choose: Surviving the Climate Crisis.* New York: Alfred A. Knopf.

Figueroa, Robert M. Indigenous Peoples and Cultural Losses. In *The Oxford Handbook of Climate Change and Society*, edited by John D. Dryzek, Richard B. Norgaard, and David Schlosberg. Pp. 232-247. Oxford: Oxford University Press.

Fleming, David. 2016. *Surviving the Future: Culture, Carnival and Capital in the Aftermath of the Market Economy*, edited by Shaun Chamberlin. White River Junction, Vermont: Chelsea Green Publishing.

Foer, Jonathan Safran. 2019. *We Are the Weather: Saving the Planet Begins at Breakfast.* New York: Farrar, Strauss and Giroux.

Ford, Tiffany, Sarah Reber, and Richard V. Reeves. 2020. Race Gaps in COVID-19 Deaths are Even Bigger Than They Appear. *Brookings Institution*, June 16, 2020. https://www.brookings.edu/blog/up-front/2020/06/16/race-gaps-in-covid-19-deaths-are-even-bigger-than-they-appear/ (accessed October 2, 2020).

Forster, Piers M., Harriet I. Forster, Mat J. Evans, Matthew J. Gidden, Chris D. Jones, Christoph A. Keller, Robin D. Lamboll, et al. 2020. Current and Future Global Climate Impacts Resulting from COVID-19. *Nature Climate Change* 10(10):913-919.

Foundation for Intentional Community. 2019. Communities Directory, Criteria. www.ic.org/policies (accessed Oct. 23, 2020).

Friedrich, Johannes, Mengpin Ge, and Andrew Pickens. 2020. This Interactive Chart Shows Changes in the World's Top 10 Emitters. World Resources Institute, Dec 10, 2020. https://www.wri.org/ insights/interactive-chart-shows-changes-worlds-top-10-emitters (accessed August 2, 201).

Fuentes, Rolando, Marzio Galeotti, Alessandro Lanza, and Baltasar Manzano. 2020. COVID-19 and Climate Change: A Tale of Two Global Problems. *Sustainability* 12(20):8560.

Gearey, Mary, and Neil Ravenscroft. 2019. The Nowtopia of the Riverbank: Elder Environmental Activism. *Nature and Space* 2(3):451-464.

Gibson-Graham, J.K. 2008. Diverse Economies: Performative Practices for "Other Worlds." *Progress in Human Geography* 32(5):613–632.

Gibson-Graham, J.K., Jenny Cameron, and Stephen Healy. 2013. *Take Back the Economy: An Ethical Guide for Transforming our Communities*. Minneapolis: University of Minnesota Press.

Gold, Russell. 2014. *The Boom: How Fracking Ignited the American Energy Revolution and Changed the World*. New York: Simon and Schuster.

Goodman, Amy. 2016. Justice and Accountability are Necessary to End Tension over Killings by Police: Interview with Cornel West. *Democracy Now*, July 18, 2016. https://www.democracynow.org/ 2016/7/18/prof_cornel_west_justice_and_accountability (accessed July 28, 2021).

Gould, Stephen J. 1994. *Eight Little Piggies: Reflections in Natural History*. New York: W.W. Norton and Company.

Gudynas, Eduardo. 2011. Buen Vivir: Today's Tomorrow. *Development* 54(4):441-447.

Gudynas, Eduardo, and Alberto Acosta. 2011. El Buen Vivir Mas Alla del Desarrollo. *Revista Quehacer* 181:70-83

Gumbel, Andrew. 2020. When Democracy Becomes Something Else: The Problem of Elections and What to Do About It. In *Democracy Unchained: How to Rebuild Government for the People*, edited by David W. Orr, Andrew Gumbel, Bakari Kitwana, and William S. Becker. Pp. 58-71. New York: The New Press.

Gray, Peter. 2013. *Free to Learn*. New York: Basic Books.

Haag, Matthew. 2018. How New Yorkers Want to Change the Streetscape for Good. *New York Times*, December 18, 2020. https://www.nytimes.com/interactive/2020/12/17/nyregion/nyc-open-streets.html?.?mc=aud_dev&ad-keywords=auddevgate&gclid= CjwKCAjwr56IBhAvEiwA1fuqGuHnqv1fRp6mydXEL7mpZf5HV-hH2421h2ndLVKMyN4Nf8Z2t-QkYBoCSuMQAvD_BwE&gclsrc =aw.ds (accessed July 14, 2021).

Hansen, James, Pushker Kharecha, Makiko Sato, Valerie Masson-Delmotte, Frank Ackerman, David J. Beerling, Paul J. Hearty, et al. 2013. Assessing "Dangerous Climate Change": Required Reduction of Carbon Emissions to Protect Young People, Future Generations, and Nature. *PLOS One* 8(12):e81648.

Harvey, David. 2000. *Spaces of Hope*. Berkeley: University of California Press.

Hawken, Paul, ed. 2017. *Drawdown: The Most Comprehensive Plan Ever Proposed to Reverse Global Warming*. New York: Penguin.

Heffron, Raphael J., and Darren McCauley. 2018. What is the "Just Transition"? *Geoforum* 88:74-77.

Helliwell, John F., Richard Layard, and Jeffrey D. Sachs. 2019. *World Happiness Report 2019*. New York: Sustainable Development

Solutions Network. https://worldhappiness.report/ed/2019/#read (accessed February 2, 2021).

Henfrey, Tom, and Justin Kenrick. 2015. *Climate, Commons and Hope: The Transition Movement in Global Perspective.* Amsterdam, Netherlands: Transnational Institute.

Henriques, Martha. 2020. Will Covid-19 Have a Lasting Impact on the Environment? *BBC*, March 27, 2020. https://www.bbc.com/future/article/20200326-covid-19-the-impact-of-coronavirus-on-the-environment (accessed March 29, 2020).

Henry, Matthew S., Morgan D. Bazilian, and Chris Markuson. 2020. Just Transitions: Histories and Futures in a Post-COVID World. *Energy Research and Social Science* 68:101668.

Hine, Dougald. 2019. Negotiating Surrender. In *This is Not a Drill: The Extinciton Rebellion Handbook*, edited by Clare Farrell, Alison Green, Sam Knights, and William Skeaping. Pp. 81-87. London: Penguin.

Hitchler, Lenore. 2018. Lawns are an Ecological Catastrophe. *ONE: Only Natural Energy*, October 3, 2018. https://www.onlynaturalenergy.com/grass-lawns-are-an-ecological-catastrophe/ (accessed June 19, 2021).

Hobson, Katherine. 2020. What Are Reggio Emilia Schools? *New York Times*, April 19, 2020. https://www.nytimes.com/2020/04/19/parenting/reggio-emilia-preschool.html (accessed February 16, 2021).

Holmgren, David. 2010. *Permaculture: Principles and Pathways Beyond Sustainability*. East Meon, UK: Permanent Publications.

Hopkins, Rob. 2008. *The Transition Handbook*: From Oil Dependency to Local Resilience. Totnes, UK: Green Books

Hopkins, Rob. 2011. *The Transition Companion: Making Your Community More Resilient in Uncertain Times.* White River Junction, Vermont: Chelsea Green Publishing.

Hopkins, Rob. 2013. *The Power of Just Doing Stuff: How Local Action Can Change the World.* Cambridge, UK: Green Books.

Hopkins, Rob. 2019. *From What Is to What If: Unleashing the Power of Imagination to Create the Future We Want*. White River Junction, Vermont: Chelsea Green Publishing.

Horowitz, Juliana Menasce, Ruth Igielnik, and Rakesh Kochhar. 2020. *Trends in Income and Wealth Inequality*. Pew Research Center. https://www.pewsocialtrends.org/2020/01/09/trends-in-income-and-wealth-inequality/ (accessed Feb 3, 2021).

IFA (International Fertilizer Association). 2016. *The Role of Fertilizers in Climate-Smart Agriculture, Contribution to the UN Climate Change Conference in Marrakesh–COP22/CMP12*. https://www.fertilizer.org/images/Library_Downloads/2016_The_Role _of_Fertilizers_in_Climate-Smart_Agriculture.pdf (accessed January 4, 2021).

IPCC. 2018. *Global Warming of 1.5°C: An IPCC Special Report on the Impacts of Global Warming of 1.5°C Above Pre-Industrial Levels and Related Global Greenhouse Gas Emission Pathways, in the Context of Strengthening the Global Response to the Threat of Climate Change, Sustainable Development, and Efforts to Eradicate Poverty*. https://www.ipcc.ch/sr15/ (accessed September 6, 2019).

Jackson, Wes. 2011. *Consulting the Genius of the Place: An Ecological Approach to a New Agriculture*. Berkeley, California: Counterpoint Press.

Johanisova, Nadia, and Marketa Vinkelhoferova. 2019. Social Solidarity Economy. In *Pluriverse: A Post-Development Dictionary*, edited by Ashish Kithari, Ariel Selleh, Arturo Escobar, Federico Demaria, and Alberto Acosta. Pp. 311-314. New Delhi, India: Tulika Books.

Jonas, Matt. 2020. Cleaner Air: The Environmental Impacts of Gas Lawn Mowers. Center for Environmental Transformation, February 3, 2020. https://www.cfet.org/cleaner-air-the-environmental-impacts-of-gas-lawn-mowers/ (accessed June 19, 2021).

Kallias, Giorgos, and Hug March. 2015. Imaginaries of Hope: The Utopianism of Degrowth. *Annals of the Association of American Geographers* 105(2):360-368.

Kellert, Stephen R. 2011. Dimensions, Elements, and Attributes of Biophilic Design. In *Biophilic Design: The Theory, Science and Practice of Bringing Buildings to Life*, edited by Stephen R.

Kellert, Judith Heerwagen, and Martin Mador. Pp. 3-19. Hoboken, New Jersey: John Wiley and Sons.

King, Martin Luther, Jr. 2018. *Letter from Birmingham Jail*. London: Penguin Classics.

Klein, Naomi. 2014. *This Changes Everything: Capitalism vs. The Climate*. New York: Simon and Schuster.

Klein, Naomi. 2019. *On Fire: The (Burning) Case for a Green New Deal*. New York: Simon and Schuster.

Kolb, David A. 2015. *Experiential Learning: Experience as the Source of Learning and Development, Second Edition*. Upper Saddle River, New Jersey: Pearson Education.

Kudryavtsev, Alex, Marianne E. Krasny, and Richard C. Stedman. 2012. The Impact of Environmental Education on Sense Off Place Among Urban Youth. *Ecosphere* 3(4):1-15.

Kusnetz, Nicholas. 2020. The Oil Market May Have Tanked, but Companies Are Still Giving Plenty to Keep Republicans in Office. Inside Climate News, October 28, 2020. https://insideclimatenews.org/news/28102020/oil-campaign-contributions-republicans-trump/ (accessed February 1, 2022).

Lal, Rattan. 2004. Soil Carbon Sequestration Impacts on Global Climate Change and Food Security. *Science* 304(5677):1623-1627.

Lawson, Willow. 2006. Study: Lawn Mowing Equals Car Trip. ABC News, January 7, 2006. https://abcnews.go.com/Technology/story?id=98532&page=1 (accessed June 17, 2021).

Lee, Martha F. 1996. *The Nation of Islam: An American Millenarian Movement*. Syracuse, New York: Syracuse University Press.

Li, Minqi. 2009. Capitalism, Climate Change and the Transition to Sustainability: Alternative Scenarios for the US, China and the

World. *Development and Change* 40(6):1039-1061.

Liu, Eric, and Scott Noppe-Brandon. 2009. *Imagination First: Unlocking the Power of Possibility*. San Francisco: John Wiley and Sons.

Lockyer, Joshua, and James R. Veteto. 2013. Environmental Anthropology Engaging Ecotopia: An Introduction. In *Environmental Anthropology Engaging Ecotopia: Bioregionalism, Permaculture, and Ecovillages,* edited by Joshua Lockyer and James R. Veteto Pp. 1-31. New York: Berghahn Books.

Lockyer, Joshua. 2017. Community, Commons, and Degrowth at Dancing Rabbit Ecovillage. *Journal of Political Ecology* 24(1):519-542.

Louv, Richard. 2008. *Last Child in the Woods: Saving Our Children from Nature-Deficit Disorder*. Chapel Hill, North Carolina: Algonquin Books.

Lovins, Amory. 2011. *Reinventing Fire: Bold Business Solutions for the New Energy Era*. White River Junction, Vermont: Chelsea Green Publishing.

Maeckelbergh, Marianne. 2009. *The Will of the Many: How the Alterglobalisation Movement is Changing the Face of Democracy*. London: Pluto Press.

Maeckelbergh, Marianne. 2011. Doing is Believing: Prefiguration as Strategic Practice in the Slterglobalization Movement. *Social Movement Studies* 10(1):1-20.

Mann, Geoff, and Joel Wainwright. 2018. *Climate Leviathan: A Political Theory of Our Planetary Future*. New York: Verso.

Mansbridge, Jane. 2012. Everyday Activism. In *The Wiley-Blackwell Encyclopedia of Social and Political Movements*, edited by David A. Snow, Donatella Della Porta, P. G. Klandermans, and Doug McAdam. Pp. 437-438. Malden, Massachusetts: Wiley-Blackwell.

Manzanedo, Rubén D., and Peter Manning. 2020. COVID-19: Lessons for the Climate Change Emergency. *Science of the Total Environment* 742:140563.

Marino, Elizabeth. 2015. *Fierce Climate, Sacred Ground: An Ethnography of Climate Change in Shishmaref, Alaska.* Fairbanks: University of Alaska Press.

Martindale, Leigh. 2015. Understanding Humans in the Anthropocene: Finding Answers in Geoengineering and Transition Towns. *Environment and Planning D: Society and Space* 33(5): 907-924.

Mayer, Jane. 2017. *Dark Money: The Hidden History of the Billionaires Behind the Rise of the Radical Right.* New York: Anchor Books.

McMullen, Ann. 2004. "Canny About Conflict": Nativism, Revitalization, and the Invention of Tradition in Native Southeastern New England. In *Reassessing Revitalization Movements: Perspectives from North America and the Pacific Islands*, edited by Michael E. Harkin. Pp. 261-277. Lincoln: University of Nebraska Press.

Mead, Margaret. 2005. *The World Ahead: An Anthropologist Anticipates the Future*, edited and with an introduction by Robert B. Textor. New York: Berghahn.

Meadows, Donella H., Dennis L. Meadows, Jorgen Randers, and William W. Behrens. 1972. *The Limits to Growth (Report to the Club of Rome).* New York: Universe Books.

Metcalf, William James. 2012. Utopian Struggle: Preconceptions and Realities of Intentional Communities. In Realizing Utopia: Ecovillage Endeavors and Academic Approaches. *Rachel Carson Center Perspectives* 8:21-29.

Mollison, Bill. 1988. *Permaculture: A Designers Manua*l. New South Wales, Australia: Tagari Press.

Montgomery, David R. 2017. *Growing a Revolution: Bringing Our Soil Back to Life.* New York: W.W. Norton and Company.

Morena, Edouard, Dunja Krause, and Dimitris Stevis, eds. 2020. *Just Transitions: Social Justice in the Shift Towards a Low-Carbon World.* London: Pluto Press.

Nash, Linda. 2006. *Inescapable Ecologies: A History of Environment, Disease, and Knowledge.* Berkeley: University of California Press.

Nikiforuk, Andrew. 2010. *Tar Sands: Dirty Oil and the Future of a Continent.* Vancouver, British Columbia: Greystone Books.

North, Anna. 2020. Every Aspect of the Coronavirus Pandemic Exposes America's Devastating Inequalities. *Vox Media,* April 10, 2020. https://www.vox.com/2020/4/10/21207520/coronavirus-deaths-economy-layoffs-inequality-covid-pandemic (accessed August 1, 2021).

North, Peter. 2014. Ten Square Miles Surrounded by Reality? Materialising Alternative Economies Using Local Currencies. *Antipode* 46(1):246–265.

North, Peter. 2019. Alternative Currencies. In *Pluriverse: A Post-Development Dictionary,* edited by Ashish Kithari, Ariel Selleh, Arturo Escobar, Federico Demaria, and Alberto Acosta. Pp. 92-95. New Delhi, India: Tulika Books.

Nuttall, Mark. 2020. Water, Ice, and Climate Change in Northwest Greenland. *Wiley Interdisciplinary Reviews: Water* 7(3):e1433.

Orr, David W. 2009. *Down to the Wire: Confronting Climate Collapse.* Oxford: Oxford University Press.

Orr, David W. 2020. Introduction. In *Democracy Unchained: How to Rebuild Government for the People,* edited by David W. Orr, Andrew Gumbel, Bakari Kitwana, and William S. Becker. Pp. 1-14. New York: The New Press.

Pepper, David. 2005. Utopianism and Environmentalism. *Environmental Politics* 14(1):3-22.

Perron, Jennifer, and Samantha Gross. 2020. Amid COVID-19, Don't Ignore the Links Between Poor Air Quality and Public Health.

Brookings Institution, August 19, 2020. https://www.brookings.edu/blog/planetpolicy/2020/08/19/amid-covid-19-dont-ignore-the-links-between-poor-air-quality-and-public-health/ (accessed October 2, 2020).

Polk, Emily. 2015. *Communicating Global to Local Resiliency: A Case Study of the Transition Movement.* Lanham, Maryland: Lexington Books.

Pollan, Michael. 2013. *Food Rules: An Eater's Manual.* New York: Penguin Group.

Pollan, Michael. 2017. Why Bother? In *Drawdown: The Most Comprehensive Plan Ever Proposed to Reverse Global Warming,* edited by Paul Hawken. Pp. 52-53. New York: Penguin.

Rankine, Claudia. 2014. *Citizen.* Minneapolis, Minnesota: Graywolf Press.

Rich, Nathaniel. 2018. Losing Earth: The Decade We Almost Stopped Climate Change. *New York Times Magazine*, August 1, 2018. https://www.nytimes.com/interactive/2018/08/01/magazine/climate-change-losing-earth.html (accessed January 18, 2022).

Rifkin, Jeremy. 2019. *The Green New Deal: Why the Fossil Fuel Civilization Will Collapse by 2028, and the Bold Economic Plan to Save Life on Earth.* New York: St. Martin's Press.

Riley, Gina. 2020. *Unschooling: Exploring Learning Beyond the Classroom.* Cham, Switzerland: Springer Nature.

Robbins, Joel. 2004. The Globalization of Pentecostal and Charismatic Christianity. *Annual Review of Anthropology* 33:117-143.

Robbins, Paul. 2007. *Lawn People: How Grasses, Weeds, and Chemicals Make Us Who We Are.* Philadelphia: Temple University Press.

Robinson, Mary. 2018. *Climate Justice: Hope, Resilience, and the Fight for a Sustainable Future.* New York: Bloomsbury.

Román-Palacios, Cristian, and John J. Wiens. 2020. Recent Responses to Climate Change Reveal the Drivers of Species Extinction and Survival. *Proceedings of the National Academy of Sciences* 117(8):4211-4217.

Roszak, Theodore. 2001. *The Voice of the Earth: An Exploration of Ecopsychology*. Grand Rapids, MI: Phanes Press.

Sargent, Lyman Tower. 2010. *Utopianism: A Very Short Introduction*. Oxford: Oxford University Press.

Sargisson, Lucy. 2007. Strange Places: Estrangement, Utopianism, and Intentional Communities. *Utopian Studies* 18(3):393-424.

Schlosberg, David, and Romand Coles. 2016. The New Environmentalism of Everyday Life: Sustainability, Material Flows and Movements. *Contemporary Political Theory* 15(2):160-181.

Schlosberg, David, and Lisette B. Collins. 2014. From Environmental to Climate Justice: Climate Change and the Discourse of Environmental Justice. *Wiley Interdisciplinary Reviews: Climate Change* 5(3):359-374.

Schumacher, Ernst Friedrich. 1973. *Small is Beautiful: A Study of Economics as if People Mattered*. New York: Vintage Books.

Sitrin, Marina. 2006. Introduction. In *Horizontalism: Voices of Popular Power in Argentina*, edited by Marina Sitrin. Pp. 1-20. Oakland, California: AK press.

Smith, Adam. 2010 [1776]. *The Wealth of Nations: An Inquiry into the Nature and Causes of the Wealth of Nations*. Petersfield, Hampshire, UK: Harriman House Limited.

Solnit, Rebecca. 2009. *A Paradise Built in Hell: The Extraordinary Communities That Arise in Disaster*. New York: Penguin.

Staples, Brent. 1986. Just Walk on By: Black Men and Public Space. *Harper's Magazine*, December 1986. Pp. 19-20.

Steffen, Will. 2011. A Truly Complex and Diabolical Policy Problem. In *The Oxford Handbook of Climate Change and Society*, edited by John S. Dryzek, Richard B. Norgaard, and David Schlosberg. Pp. 31-37. Oxford: Oxford University Press.

Steffen, Will, Wendy Broadgate, Lisa Deutsch, Owen Gaffney, and Cornelia Ludwig. 2015. The Trajectory of the Anthropocene: The Great Acceleration. *The Anthropocene Review* 2(1):81-98.

Steffen, Will, Katherine Richardson, Johan Rockström, Sarah E. Cornell, Ingo Fetzer, Elena M. Bennett, Reinette Biggs et al. 2015. Planetary Boundaries: Guiding Human Development on a Changing Planet. *Science* 347(6223):736.

Steffen, Will, Johan Rockström, Katherine Richardson, Timothy M. Lenton, Carl Folke, Diana Liverman, Colin P. Summerhayes, et al. 2018. Trajectories of the Earth System in the Anthropocene. *Proceedings of the National Academy of Sciences* 115(33):8252-8259.

Tate, Julie, Jennifer Jenkin, and Steven Rich. 2021. Police Shootings Continue Daily, Despite a Pandemic, Protests and Pushes for Reform. *Washington Post*, August 12, 2021. https://www.washingtonpost.com/investigations/interactive/2021/police-shootings-since-2015 (accessed August 12, 2021).

Taylor, Dorceta. 2014. *Toxic Communities: Environmental Racism, Industrial Pollution, and Residential Mobility*. New York: NYU Press.

Thorp, Laurie. 2006. *The Pull of the Earth: Participatory Ethnography in the School Garden.* Lanham, Maryland: Altamira Press.

Toledo, Victor M. 2019. Agroecology. In *Pluriverse: A Post-Development Dictionary*, edited by Ashish Kithari, Ariel Selleh, Arturo Escobar, Federico Demaria, and Alberto Acosta. Pp. 85-88. New Delhi, India: Tulika Books.

Tokar, Brian. 2020. Climate Justice and Community Renewal: An Introduction. In *Climate Justice and Community Renewal: Resistance and Grassroots Solutions,* edited by Brian Tokar and Tamra Gilbertson. Pp. 1-16. Milton Park, Oxon, UK: Routledge.

Tuck, Eve. 2009. Suspending Damage: A Letter to Communities. *Harvard Educational Review* 79(3):409-428.

United States Environmental Protection Agency. No date. Sources of Greenhouse Gas Emissions. https://www.epa.gov/ghgemissions/sources-greenhouse-gas-emissions (accessed July 28, 2021).

Veteto, James R. and Joshua Lockyer. 2013. Environmental Anthropology Engaging Permaculture; Moving Theory and Practice Toward Sustainability. In *Environmental Anthropology Engaging Ecotopia: Bioregionalism, Permaculture, and Ecovillages,* edited by Joshua Lockyer and James R. Veteto Pp. 95-112. New York: Berghahn Books.

Wahl, Daniel. 2016. *Designing Regenerative Cultures*. Axminster, UK: Triarchy Press.

Wallace, Anthony F.C. 1956. Revitalization Movements. *American Anthropologist* 58(2):264-281.

Wallace, Anthony F.C. 2004. Foreword. In *Reassessing Revitalization Movements: Perspectives from North American and the Pacific Islands*, edited by Michael E. Harkin. Pp. vii-xi. Lincoln: University of Nebraska Press.

Weart, Spencer. 2011. The Development of the Concept of Dangerous Anthropogenic Climate Change. In *The Oxford Handbook of Climate Change and Society*, edited by John D. Dryzek, Richard B. Norgaard, and David Schlosberg. Pp. 67-81. Oxford: Oxford University Press.

Welch, Craig. 2019. Climate Change Has Finally Caught Up to This Alaska Village. *National Geographic*, October 22, 2019. https://www.nationalgeographic.com/science/article/climate-change-finally-caught-up-to-this-alaska-village (accessed March 25, 2021).

Whitney, Daniel G., and Mark D. Peterson. 2019. US National and State-Level Prevalence of Mental Health Disorders and Disparities of Mental Health Care Use in Children. *JAMA Pediatrics* 174(4):389-391.

Wilber, Tom. 2012. *Under the Surface: Fracking, Fortunes, and the Fate of the Marcellus Shale*. Ithaca, New York: Cornell University Press.

Williams, Florence. 2016. This Is Your Brain on Nature. *National Geographic* 229(1):48-69.

Willow, Anna J. 2018. *Understanding ExtrACTIVISM: Culture and Power in Natural Resource Disputes.* London: Routledge.

Willow, Anna J. 2021. Transition as Cultural Revitalization: Exploring Social Motives for Environmental Movement Participation. *Nature and Culture* 16(2):13-41.

Wilson, Edward O. 1984. *Biophilia: The Human Bond with Other Species*. Cambridge, Maryland: Harvard University Press.

Wu, Xiao, Rachel C. Nethery, Benjamin M. Sabath, Danielle Braun, and Francesca Dominici. 2020. Exposure to Air Pollution and COVID-19 Mortality in the United States. *Science Advances* 6(45):eabd4049.

Yates, Luke. 2015. Rethinking Prefiguration: Alternatives, Micropolitics and Goals in Social Movements. *Social Movement Studies* 14(1):1-21.

Zarger, Becky. 2008. School Garden Pedagogies: Understanding Childhood Landscapes. *Anthropology News* 49(4):8-9.

Index